Evening

Number 24, Summer 2020

...all men and women are created equal in rights to life, liberty, and the pursuit of happiness.

—Elizabeth Cady Stanton, revision of the American Declaration of Independence, 1848

Published Twice (or More) a Year
by
Evening Street Press

Editor & Managing Editor: Barbara Bergmann
Associate Editors: Donna Spector, Kailen Nourse-Driscoll, Patti Sullivan, Anthony Mohr, L D Zane, Stacia Levy, Jeffrey Davis, Dana Stamps II

Founding Editor: Gordon Grigsby

Evening Street Review is published in the spring and fall of every year (with additional issues as needed) by Evening Street Press. United States subscription rates are $24 for two issues and $44 for four issues (individuals), and $32 for two issues and $52 for four issues (institutions).

Cover art by Patti Sullivan

Library of Congress Control Number:2020930036

ISBN: 978-1-937347-56-7

Evening Street Review is centered on the belief that all men and women are created equal, that they have a natural claim to certain inalienable rights, and that among these are the rights to life, liberty, and the pursuit of happiness. With this center, and an emphasis on writing that has both clarity and depth, it practices the widest eclecticism. Evening Street Review reads submissions of poetry (free verse, formal verse, and prose poetry) and prose (short stories and creative nonfiction) year round. Submit 3-6 poems or 1-2 prose pieces at a time. Payment is one contributor's copy. Copyright reverts to author upon publication. Response time is 3-6 months. Please address submissions to Editors, 2881 Wright St, Sacramento, CA 95821-4819. Email submissions are also acceptable; send to the following address as Microsoft Word or rich text files (.rtf): **editor@eveningstreetpress.com**.

For submission guidelines, subscription information, published works, and author profiles, please visit our website: **www.eveningstreetpress.com**.

© Copyright 2020 by Evening Street Press
2881 Wright St
Sacramento, CA 95821
All rights revert to the author upon publication.

Photo: www.smithsonianmag.com/smithsonian-institution/these-haunting-red-dresses-memorialize-murdered-and-missing-indigenous-women-180971730/

"1 in 3 American Indian and Alaska Native women will be raped, but survivors rarely find justice on tribal lands" Oct. 18, 2019

USA Today Editor's note: Over the course of an 18-month investigation into prosecutions of sexual assault on tribal lands, Newsy reporters uncovered breakdowns in the federal and tribal criminal justice systems so severe that sexual perpetrators often received minimal or no punishment and survivors were left with little justice. The full documentary, titled "A Broken Trust," is available here.
www.youtube.com/watch?v=-slFVM4ECUk&feature=youtu.be

In *"A Broken Trust"* at minute 22:

If a tribal court convicts (tribal courts cannot prosecute non-tribal members), the maximum sentence is one year (or just recently 3) while similar cases outside the reservation can be up to 100 years. Federal convictions could have higher sentences, but are rarely taken up by the courts.

www.usatoday.com/story/news/nation/2019/10/18/native-american-women-sexual-assault-justice-issue-tribe-lands/3996873002/

EVENING STREET REVIEW
PUBLISHED BY EVENING STREET PRESS

NUMBER 24, SUMMER 2020

CONTENTS

BY THE EDITOR	(In)justice	6
JAMES DOYLE	Are You Kidding? Inside front cover, 166, and back cover	

POETRY

JAMES FOWLER	Buddha Squirrels	7
	The Twelve Labors of Hercules	7
	Company Town	9
STEPHEN BOULHOSA	Team Colors	19
	Rude Awakening	21
MEREDITH DAVIES HADAWAY	October: the Week in Review	29
	Vigil	29
STEVEN BEAUCHAMP	Tybee Revisited	30
JOHN KRUMBERGER	Spilled Milk	32
ARTHUR GINSBERG	On a Perspective of Things	33
	The Bones are Singing	34
	Election	35
	X-mas Heart-string	36
ZACK ROGOW	Getting Personal	47
	To the Person Who had Me Ticketed for Blocking His Driveway	48
HOLLY DAY	The Tree in Our Back Yard	49
DEBORAH FLEMING	Chemistry Poem	59
	Prophet	60
AARON PARKER	Live A Cide	61
HIROMI YOSHIDA	TV Dinner	72
JEAN VARDA	Drops of Mercy	73
ALEXANDER PAYNE MORGAN	Bistro Savannah	79
	Bus Station Prayer	80
	Persistence	81
	Ode to Blueberries	83
BRAD G GARBER	Dash Naked	93
	Great American	94
WILL WALKER	Constitutional	101
DAVID JAMES	Ars Poetica: Kroger's on Grand River	102

EDWARD RIELLY	A Departure	105
IAIN MACDONALD	*Burn Your Journal*	106
STEVEN PELCMAN	On the Tenth Anniversary of a Husband's Death	118
	Neighbors	119
SUSAN TOLLEFSON	Alloy Prayer	127
W LUTHER JETT	The Busboy	127
ELIZABETH WEIR	Intermission at Lee Blessing's, "Going to St. Ives"	132
	At San Francisco Airport	132
ELAINE COHEN	You Can't Go Home Again	133
MICHAEL MINASSIAN	Compassion's Carriage	138
	How to Write a Poem	139
JOHN GREY	Regarding my Time Spent in the Choir	140
PAULA YUP	Milk Bottle	152
	Cinco de Mayo	153
ALISON STONE	Friends are Starting to do Stuff to their Faces	156

FICTION

TESSA SMITH MCGOVERN	For Better or for Worse	31
J F CONNOLLY	Bayonne	50
ROBERT GRANADER	Curable	61
ELIZABETH STANDING BEAR	Holly Patterson	85
MARTHA K DAVIS	Wild Kingdom	95
HAVA THOMPSON KOHL-RIGGS	What's Eggs Got to Do with It	103
GLEN WEISSENBERGER	Stops along the Way	106
LINDSEY ANDERSON	Acadia	120
WILLIAM THOMPSON	The Book Finder	128
PHIL MERSHON	White Church	141
TAMRA WILSON	Steve's Ashes	154
MARGARET HERMES	The Off-Season	157

NONFICTION

MICHAEL COHEN	The Hand in the Glove	11
JAN SHOEMAKER	Through the Trees	22
PAUL C DALMAS	Never Held a Basketball	37
PETER BREYER	Fifty-Two Years Later	74
TIM MENEES	House Tour	134

CONTRIBUTORS	159

(IN)JUSTICE

Perhaps it was inevitable that our DIY Prison Project would lead to a discussion of the death penalty. To place it in perspective, the Trump Administration announced that it will be carrying out executions; the governor of California suspended executions.

Now we have a non-fiction work from a prisoner on death row who claims that death is the more humane punishment than life without parole. Here are the comments from our DIY associate editor: "[This piece] created a lot of drama for us. I think that it is a difficult idea to communicate to anyone who hasn't done a lot of time. It is a difficult idea to accept for some of us who have. The table turned loud and angry.

"I think that it is very easy to say, 'Don't do the crime if you can't do the time.' That phrase inoculates citizens against compassion. It promotes mistreatment from security. It accepts under-treatment and malpractice from medical staff, and mega-sentences from judges that tally the hundreds of thousands of years every election season."

In the meantime, the discussion over whether the death penalty is cruel or unusual punishment is being debated, largely outside prison walls.

We have condensed the argument for the death penalty for this issue of the Review (beginning on the inside front cover): the full version can be found on our web page: https://eveningstreetpress.com/diy-prison-project.html

Meanwhile, prison conditions of truly cruel proportions are being revealed in the press. This contrasts with the ability of writers in some prisons to create and distribute their work.

In another question of (in)justice, indigenous women and girls are disproportionally victims of sexual violence and trafficking, to a certain extent because there is little chance of prosecution of their tormentors. Even if a conviction is obtained, if it is a tribal member, the maximum sentence is one year (recently extended to the possibility of three years). In contrast, if the conviction were outside tribal lands, sentences go as high as 100 years. If the perpetrator is a non-tribal member, the federal government rarely prosecutes, and the tribes cannot try non-tribal members for any crime.*

Our nation needs to reassess its justice system including stakeholders in the discussion: harsh punishment, no consequences, and the prohibition of native tribes to control what happens on their own lands.

*usatoday.com/story/news/nation/2019/10/18/native-american-women-sexual-assault-justice-issue-tribe-lands/3996873002/

BB

JAMES FOWLER
BUDDHA SQUIRRELS

They sit on their haunches,
little paws on their paunches,
and pass beyond acorn and cat.

For all of their hoarding,
their scampering and scolding,
they aspire to be more than just fat.

THE TWELVE LABORS OF HERCULES

First, find the missing sock. Eureka: down the pant leg.

Next he must scrape gum from the underside of things.
Nearly driven mad, he wrecks gum factories far and wide.

His third labor has him correcting apostrophe usage.
No, you fools. It's a simple plural, not a possessive.
Egged on by nuns, he raps knuckles with his club.

The fourth allows him some creative latitude:
illustrate a stretch-from-Earth-to-moon analogy.
He stacks cargo containers. With the cargo still inside.
Consumers howl over the sudden shortage of electronics.

Number five: audit the books of a multinational
playing a shell game with profits. Not being good
at math, he hauls Cerberus into the boardroom
and lobs the heads of three smirking executives
down its gullets. A spirit of cooperation prevails.

Now he must judge a beauty contest. *Too skinny*,
he grumbles. Miss Caucasus Mountains isn't bad.
His questions catch the contestants off guard.
What would you do if abducted by a Centaur?
Would you mind a Nemean lion throw on your bridal bed?
How might you protect your babies from serpents?   (cont)

For his seventh task he is to set a new world record.
Puzzling a moment, he suddenly issues a keen whistle
and the sky darkens with an old foe, Stymphalian birds.
As if fed through a chute, the birds pass between his hands
and arc upward, until the whole flock has been juggled
into a huge bird wheel as large as the London Eye.
PETA objects, so the feat isn't added to the Guinness rolls.

The eighth labor: clean up an oil spill in the Gulf.
After scooping all the sand off coastal beaches,
he shovels it onto the slick, then hauls the sticky mess
to Canada, dumping it on the other oil sands. Recycling.
Then, flanked by Miss Sri Lanka, the pageant winner
whose mongoose answer to the serpent question he liked,
he restores the beaches by pulverizing boulders with
his bare hands, flexing all the while for the cameras.

Not being a modern man, he says the ninth task
irks him: garner a billion Likes on social media.
Popularity has never been a priority for him,
but his previous exploits have already put him past
the 500 million mark. Disdaining kittens and puppies,
he decides to go for broke in the stupid-stunts category.
His Goldberg variation (Rube) involves a trireme,
a catapult, a statue of Apollo, ping pong balls, plastique,
and a wall of paint cans. What's not to like?

When told he must next split the atom with
a length of hose, he recalls a drunken conversation
with Democritus and suspects he is being asked
to do the impossible. A group of Aristotle types
assure him it can be done, but chuckle at the hose bit.
In the lab he wants to know which atom exactly,
so they draw a small arrow on the table top.
With lightning speed he slaps the spot with the hose,
producing a concussion blast that vaporizes the table.
Split enough for you? he inquires of the staggered Aristotles.

(cont)

He laughs at the eleventh task: world peace
for a year. Like himself, he assumes men enjoy
using muscle to get their way. Of course,
Ares is a bloody bastard who needs some reining.
So peace it is, but the only kind that holds is backed
by force. Bribing him with Hippolyta's girdle and
orthotic supports, Hercules recruits Atlas, whose
merest shrug can bring the heavens crashing down on
any army that breaks the peace. He calls
this arrangement Pax Herculana. It requires
no buy-in, just healthy fear of falling skies.

The final labor taxes his wits, which he does have
despite popular opinion. He is to retrieve that hope
said to lie at the bottom of Pandora's opened box.
After much searching he finds the little chest,
which seems quite empty. A passing poet says
something about wings, an Aristotle something about
a cat. Though a demigod with a passport stamped
for Olympus, he understands suffering, the weary tread
along a comfortless road. So he closes the box
and has a plaque engraved with this message:
KEEP SHUT. HEART OF HOPE INSIDE. PLACE NEXT TO EAR.
IF OPENED, EXPECT BEATING FROM ME. LOVE, HERCULES.

Fowler

COMPANY TOWN

They've named streets after product lines,
set up a chapel devoted to just profits
and lower taxes (the other denominations
in town praying on their own dime).

The company store has everything from mops
to mushrooms, at near-PX prices.
Like monthly rent for company housing,
it's all deducted for modest fees.

There's the school, where children learn
industry, assured of jobs on finishing,
or, failing that, of one-way bus tickets
to the next town over, a sink for slackers.

(cont)

The library keeps first editions of
Smith, Rand, and Friedman on display.
Just so, customized comics lead youngsters
through the evil progress of unionism

As sly recruiters dangle impossible raises
and benefits before innocent workers.
Luckily, they see through the socialist lies
just in time to defeat the ruse.

Management and labor celebrate with
handshakes and back pats all around.
"Boy, what a close call," Mike Goodman
whistles, thankful for steady employment.

Meanwhile, over at the civic theater
moviegoers emulate the plucky individual
who braves the runaway train/desert sun/
pissed-off bear/touchy dynamite/creeping gangrene.

Of course, they have the company clinic for
such things as birthing and industrial mishaps,
because the occasional silly billy *will* ignore
clearly posted warnings to work safely.

It's all proof of the cradle-to-grave
contract between freely consenting parties.
And if on Founder's Day they choose to sway
in concentric rings around the bandstand

on the town green, don't let phrases like
Hoos in Hooville denigrate the scene.
Once beyond incorporated limits, it may be
harder to part company than you suppose.

Fowler

MICHAEL COHEN
THE HAND IN THE GLOVE
based upon an excerpt from *Rivertown Heroes*

"Can you believe that story he just told, Mr. Hirsch?"

Reverend Arthur Cook has sat sphinxlike for two days of court, barely nodding to me from the time we enter the courtroom in the morning to the slam of Judge Sirica's hammer at the end of the day. Suddenly the reverend is talking to me—his lawyer, Nathan Hirsch—in a hushed tone of astonishment. His mouth is sagging open with amazement after Horace Parker, the witness and victim, finishes his testimony intended to put the reverend in jail.

I look incredulous too. For the first time in this proceeding, I am not distracted by Reverend Cook's disdain for me. If you can believe Horace Parker, tiny Reverend Cook, who is no more than the height of a Shetland pony, viciously attacked Mr. Parker—a black mountain of a man, a decorated ex-military policeman, and a uniformed government security guard. Horace has piously sworn Reverend Cook slashed him repeatedly and unrepentantly with an open-blade razor, the kind used by barbers in the '30s. Horace Parker has just rolled up his sleeves and shown the jury three knife slashes crisscrossing the back of his forearm, which is the size of a Virginia ham.

And all over a woman—Mrs. Parker, or "the missus," as Horace has just described his wife. Yesterday the jury met the weeping missus who, when sworn to testify, had no intention of confessing any greater sin than being a good churchgoer and, much to the prosecutor's dismay, refused to acknowledge that she saw the altercation between her husband and the reverend.

No question that the missus is Horace's match—she's oversize in every way. All hips and breasts swaddled in burgundy crepe, she appears to outweigh the reverend even if he were sopping wet. As nervous as this case has left me, I find myself drifting off, trying to understand taste and sex.

Reverend Cook is a reserved man, a force in the civil rights movement a decade ago. Now the same Reverend Cook, who claimed inspiration from Gandhi, looks shocked at the suggestion that he, and not Horace Parker, was the aggressor. But that is what Officer Parker has just said. He has testified that he caught the reverend kissing the missus and that the reverend pulled out an old-fashioned straightedge and sliced the officer's arm in three places. Since nobody was there with a candle, the tale of the fight between the two men is a liar's contest.

I nod to Reverend Cook in agreement and take the time to look around the courtroom to see if by chance my boss, Lynn Reilly, might accidentally appear which he has not. His absence is by design and plan conceived with and approved by the reverend. But I see he has sent Hulda Pollak, his massive secretary, to "help" me.

Hulda is an outspoken legal secretary, a dangerous old pro, and no friend of mine. She sits in the first row of visitor benches behind the barristers' tables, and no one has chosen to sit next to her. Who would? Glistening, as the Virginians refer to sweating, Hulda radiates heat, the smell of West Virginia grit, and District of Columbia contempt for everyone and everything legal.

Hulda is a spy. One screw up by me that she reports back to her boss and mine, and I am undone.

Judge Sirica, who is presiding over this trial, is also not on my side. Not one smile bends his lips. They say he was a boxer. This is surprising, for he is a tiny wizened guy with nasty crow like eyes. He peers at me only infrequently, but when he does, his eyes reflect at best boredom and at worst thinly veiled contempt.

I guess I can understand why his mind might be elsewhere. While he is down in this courtroom, he must be thinking of the Watergate grand jury upstairs that he supervises, the jurors there looking to indict half or more of President Nixon's White House team and perhaps President Nixon himself. And the *Washington Post* says Judge Sirica is a Republican. Watergate must stick in his craw.

Yesterday I saw the Watergate jurors being led like sheep past our courtroom, their "JUROR" tags dangling on chains around their necks, their faces grim. They were heading to lunch, but if you considered the serious looks in their eyes, they could have been heading to a hanging.

If I think too much about how the reverend feels about me, intermixed with Judge Sirica's indifference or contempt (I cannot tell which)—not to mention the distraction of Watergate—I will not be able to do my job. I can remember the coaching of my older brother, Ritchie, an intense athlete and competitor. Ritchie would be hammering away at me.

"Stay in the game. Focus."

I try my best, with eyes unblinking, jaw set, a modest grimace on my lips, tongue lingering in the corner of my mouth. If he were here with me, Ritchie would say that being the reverend's lawyer is no different from standing at the plate with a baseball bat on my shoulder, waiting for the next pitch.

On the witness stand, in his green museum-guard uniform, Horace Parker looks comfortable, his righteousness spreading over the jury like his girth spreading over the lip of the witness chair. He looks as if he could crush the reverend just by sitting on him.

"And they think I wasn't frightened by that figure filling up my doorway?" the reverend whispers to me. For the first time in this courtroom, the reverend angles toward me so that our knees touch, and no one can see us, much less hear us, as we talk. Reverend Cook's left eyelid perpetually droops as he whispers to me, giving him a skeptical view of me as his lawyer. This is as it should be, since he had wanted my boss, Lynn Reilly, and not me sitting next to him in court.

* * *

"In all sense and manner, Reverend," Lynn Reilly had said, pushing his thinning hair off his forehead as we sat in his DuPont Circle office, "you want the jury to see a novice representing you, an innocent face. With a smart noggin, to be sure. Because with all your character, your excellent reputation, your imposing presence, and your brilliance as a preacher, Reverend, you win on the strength of your telling of this sad episode and not on a stale recounting of the case by some counsel of lesser skill than you. No disrespect, Mr. Hirsch."

I nodded—no offense taken—but in fact my face reddened, and I gripped the chair. Now I was the counsel of lesser skill, hardly the kind of endorsement I wanted from my boss.

Lynn Reilly always speaks crisply, with a slight Maryland drawl through his buckteeth.

"Now, Mr. Hirsch here, he'll take care of the details. The jury will be on his side, the young lawyer trying to do his best. The jurors will have lowered expectations. You, Reverend, and no one else, will thrill and engage the jury with your declaration of the falsehood of Mr. Parker's story. I can assure you that the jury would be disappointed if they could not carry your words and your image into their deliberations at the case's end."

I could see the logic in my boss's strategy. This case was lock, stock, and barrel about the reverend. The jury would either believe he was innocent, a man who defended himself against an enraged husband, or find him guilty, an adulterer who failed to tell them the truth.

I was to be the fellow who simply announced that the reverend had arrived. I'd introduce him to the jury, giving him the opportunity to thunder out the truth of his innocence.

Lynn Reilly, the latest of my mentors, was always respectful. It was part of his power of persuasion. But selling me to the reverend had been an uphill battle even for Lynn Reilly, the master of the District of Columbia criminal courts. Reverend Cook's sagging eyelid told the tale, that droopy eye staring a message at me: "You mean I'm gonna have to let some white boy do a man's job?"

I prayed that my eyes did not affirm the reverend's assessment; I silently pursed my lips with seriousness to keep from an involuntary blink or two. Alas, in one flinch, I feared he had me. But I judged the reverend too swiftly.

"Mr. Reilly, you want me to put faith into your view." The reverend always speaks with a slow, deliberate musical cadence, the hallmark of his ministry. "You claim I need your guidance, your fine hand, with your representative, so to speak, doing the legwork. Well, that's fine, sir. Now you give me your hand."

I watched as the reverend reached over to grasp Lynn Reilly's hand in expectation of their bond. His requirement of commitment was unmistakable.

"I will take your Mr. Hirsch—your glove, as it were—into court with me," he says, "but I will expect you to place your hand, this hand that I now hold in mine; I expect your hand inside that glove, if you see my point. And knowing that, I'll walk into that courtroom having had the benefit of your defense. Do I have your hand in this, sir?"

The reverend had nailed me down to a T. A puppet. It must have shown that there was plenty of room for my boss's hand to push and pull me about as the protection of the reverend might demand. I realized it too. I had been emptied by the death of my older brother, Ritchie, whose life had been taken from him in a Southeast Asian rice paddy.

The thought of a world without Ritchie left me hollow and spent. He had been so vital and assured. I could see Ritchie pitching with inexhaustible velocity at the top of the ninth, watch him in full stride with a football tucked in his right arm as he stiff-armed with his left some fool who had attempted the impossible task of dragging him down alone in midfield. I could watch Ritchie's hijinks with Phil and Gene, his adoring pals, clowning around the Zesto Drive-In on a twilit summer night.

And I could hear Ritchie moaning and thrashing about as he made love to a naked girl in his hideaway crawl space above the family garage, a cave padded with old military-surplus wool blankets, unaware that he was being spied on by me, his envious thirteen-year-old brother. Ritchie was my compass, and I believe with a lawyer's conviction that I lost him forever because of what I put in motion. My loss, my doing.

* * *

I take the calming step of setting up my note cards for the cross-examination of Officer Parker. As I flip the cards, my mind begins to drift. My hold on D.C. has always felt fragile; while this place has served me as a temporary moorage, the opposing currents of my small-town family world seem to draw me back. Even as the courtroom begins to stir, I sense with resignation that those currents have yet again washed in my past.

When I close my eyes, familiar faces and whispers surround me. They are a presence from the home I left—Bethell, on the shores of Puget Sound in Washington State. I find myself involuntarily sighing; it is my permanent phantom jury, ready as always to adjust my successes downward and judge my blunders as fatal. My shoulders slump to their discomfited shuffling feet, the embarrassed clapping of hands, the disapproving grunts, raised eyebrows, and critical muttering. I try unsuccessfully to shut out their spectral judgement.

When I try to shut the Bethell jury out, it ebbs but then materializes by releasing its verdicts into the air around me, accompanied by the patter of Northwest rain on roofs and the slap of tidal waves on rocky beaches, the sounds, smells, places, and people from whom I have long tried to separate.

I awaken with a start. The courtroom is filling with functionaries, bailiffs, marshals, clerks, and assistant DAs. They raise dust motes as they open briefcases, fold newspapers, brush chair seats, and tuck coats behind them, all reaching assigned positions in the court before Judge Sirica appears. None, not even the reverend, have any idea that there will be two juries watching me cross-examine Officer Parker. One that I have appointed, one selected by Judge Sirica. I am not sure which will matter more.

On the witness stand Horace Parker is as comfortable as if he were sitting in a movie theater. I rise and approach the bar. Lynn Reilly has painstakingly drilled me on the questions I will ask.

"Mr. Parker, can I call you 'Officer'?" I ask and take a deep breath. Mrs. Jefferson, the last juror in the front row, maternally crinkles her face at me. "You're doing fine, son," her smile says, and I am momentarily heartened.

Willie Smith, the assistant DA, just smirks. The day before, during the break, when we stood in the men's room stall to stall, Willie said out loud to anyone who could hear, "I am kicking your butt." Zipping myself quickly in retreat, I thought he was right.

I am sure that as far as Willie is concerned, my examination will go right along with his direct examination establishing Officer Parker's legitimacy and decency. A security guard. A man to be honored and respected. Someone who would not lie about who attacked whom.

"Now, Officer Parker, you told the jury you served in the military before your present job in the National Gallery."

"I did." Officer Parker sits straighter, if that is possible.

"You were a military policeman, I believe."

"Yep."

"And served with distinction?"

A nod and a "Yup."

"Any awards?"

"A number of ribbons." Horace Parker tries to look humble, but he is pleased pink to be able to talk in detail about his achievements. He has a remarkable record.

"What were they for?"

"Oh, there was a stockade breakout in Korea," he says.

"Pretty serious, Officer?"

"Oh yes." Officer Parker laughs with a rumble of menace. "We had prisoners running around like escaped mice. Seven of 'em."

"Did you personally catch any?"

"Got 'em all," Horace answers with satisfaction.

"You got them all?" I appear suitably impressed. I stroll over toward the jury box, just as Lynn Reilly instructed me.

"That way, once the witness is going with you," my boss explained to me, "you have him facing the jury as he's talking to you. Then, when the high point in your examination arrives, you have the jurors looking right into his face."

Lynn Reilly is like a football coach. He calls the plays. I execute them. It's working just as he indicated it would. The jury is looking at Horace Parker.

"How exactly did you accomplish the capture, Officer?"

"I was at the door." Horace grins, his mouth cavernous. I imagine him downing a double cheeseburger in one bite. "They had to get by me to get out."

"Seven prisoners," I marvel. "What did you do to subdue that number of men?"

"I kinda used the first one as a club to knock the others out. It was like bowling." The memory makes him laugh again. I look at one of the women in the jury. Horace's laughing about his exploits at bashing people is starting to wear thin. Oblivious to sounding like a braggart, Horace loves the chance to tell his story. By now the jury must feel that this man is a force of nature—and not always a nice one.

"Officer Parker," I inquire, "are you trained in the martial arts?"

"Yessir. Judo and jujitsu." Horace's answer snaps like a salute.

"Have you kept it up?"

"Every week. Yessir."

Willie Smith, the prosecutor, looks up. He has realized that his victim just described himself to the jury as a one-man army.

"So, if I may," I ask, "back to the jailbreak in Korea. Anybody armed?"

He recites, "The usual: jail shivs, sharpened spoons. And one smuggled gun."

"And the commendation you received declares that you disarmed an entire jail wing."

"That's what it says all right." Horace shifts his weight in the witness chair, as if to put another bad guy to rest. The jurors have to be thinking how it was impossible for this man to have let the little reverend pull a razor on him.

"All the knives?" I question.

"Yessir." There's Horace's salute again.

"Were there any big guys?"

Another rumbling laugh. "Not as big as me."

"But good-size?"

Horace nods.

Now, just as Lynn Reilly had forecast, the jury has all of the facts about this formidable fighting machine. The step is for me to bring Horace's reputation home to Washington, D.C.

Some of the jurors are shifting around with nervousness. I hope they're getting worried that Officer Parker might jump over the ledge of the jury box and pounce on them next. But maybe they are just tired of me dragging this out. I have no idea which it is.

"You must be proud of the commendation," I note with respect.

"It helped get my job with the gallery," Horace concedes.

"And you were given an award at your church as well, were you not?"

"Yessir. The Harmony Baptist Church gave me a plaque at a Sunday service."

"And so everybody knew about your physical feats?"

"I suspect so," Horace answers. I can see he's getting a little uneasy about where this is going.

"Now, Officer Parker," I ask, "have there ever been any acts of violence in your neighborhood? Anybody ever robbed and assaulted?"

"Yessir. All the time. We don't get the police help we need."

I acknowledge that it's a problem by nodding my head in agreement. Horace Parker lives in a tough neighborhood.

"Officer, have you ever been robbed on the street?"

Horace laughs spontaneously. There is that booming self-confident rumble again. It is like the starting of a diesel engine with a nasty exhaust.

"Nobody that dumb gonna take me on." He grins.

"I can surely see that." I grin back. "So that experience of yours in the service—you taking out seven men—that experience was well-known, then?"

That question seems to yank the prosecutor, Willie Smith, straight out of his chair. He is positively shouting out his objection.

"Only admissible if he knows, Your Honor." Willie is agitated by Horace Parker now telling the jury that people in his neighborhood might be afraid of him. But Horace answers without waiting.

"Yessir. I think so."

"Wasn't it Reverend Cook's church where your military exploits were announced to the community?"

"Hmmm," Officer Parker says. It's all that he can say.

I marvel at Lynn Reilly's insight. "Trust me, Mr. Hirsch," Lynn had intoned, the light from his desk lamp shining into his intense face. "Mr. Parker will hobble the prosecutor's case if he acknowledges that even the reverend might have been afraid of him."

Lynn Reilly, the puppeteer, again was on target.

"So, Officer Parker," I say, "if I can summarize, you are well-known as one of the strongest men in your neighborhood, so that no one tangles with you, yes?"

"If you say so," Parker mumbles. He looks at me, and because of where I am standing, the jury can see his eyebrows knitted in anger. I wouldn't want to run into Horace in an alley after that look. Nor would the jurors. Even Horace knows he is not much of a victim anymore.

And now my penultimate question, rehearsed and rehearsed with Lynn Reilly and Reverend Cook late into the night: "Mr. Parker, could I ask you to look at Reverend Cook?"

At this question the reverend rises slowly, with great dignity, as planned, his five-foot-four frame a fraction of the size of the massive Horace Parker. I can see the eyes of two of the jury members darting back and forth, measuring the tiny alleged assailant and his gigantic judo-trained victim.

"Officer," I ask innocently, "would you say the prisoner in the Korean stockade that you picked up to knock over the other six escapees was bigger or smaller than Reverend Cook?"

My sympathetic juror, Mrs. Jefferson, openly smiles. There are giggles in the courtroom. Judge Sirica cements my cross by slamming his gavel and calling for quiet.

"You've made your point, Mr. Hirsch," the judge cautions. "Move on." But there is respect in his tone.

The jury hears his respect too. Afterward, the reverend's stem-winder testimony drives home the last nail in the coffin of the prosecutor's case. After they have returned to the jury room from a lunch at a nearby restaurant on the government's tab, the jury acquits the reverend in ten minutes.

The reverend shakes hands with the jury members, and some applaud. As we leave, I turn back to the empty courtroom, where I think I hear the phantom Bethell jury whispering among themselves, yet again not satisfied with my performance.

STEPHEN BOULHOSA
TEAM COLORS

I am a big baseball fan.
Have been for almost 50 years now.
Saw my first major league game when I was six.
Shea Stadium, Queens, NY. An afternoon affair.
The Mets vs. God Knows Who.
It was a Boy Scout trip.
My father wasn't with us that day. He was working,
so my mother accompanied me and my older brother.
He was the scout. I was the tagalong.
The troop had rented a bus
and when we pulled into the parking lot
I'm told the scoutmaster, Mr. Manning,
offered an extra ticket to our bus driver. (cont)

"Not great seats, but the price is right," Mr. Manning said.
The bus driver accepted
and into the stadium we went. The whole lot of us.
I hadn't had my heart surgery yet.
Wouldn't for another year or so, in fact.
So my mother carried me.
She did that often back then
when she didn't want me to "miss out" on things.
It was as hot as Hades in a heat wave that day
and Mr. Manning wasn't kidding about the seats.
The players on the field already looked like ants
when we got to the upper deck level
and that was *before* the usher pointed us all the way to the top.
Mr. Manning and a few of the other fathers hurried up the stairs,
looking to get the best of the worst seats in the house, I suppose.
My mother, sweat running down her face and back, stared up, daunted.
"I'll take him up, ma'am." The deep voice came from behind us.
It was our bus driver. My mother didn't argue.
And so this large black man took me from my mother's arms
and placed me on his broad shoulders.
Up he climbed, no doubt passing disapproving stares and *tsk tsks*
with my milk-white mother and brother in tow, likely doing the same.
"You're all right, I gotcha," he said a few times, reassuring me.
When we got to the top of the grandstand
he handed me off to my mother and shook my hand.
"Okay, young fella," he said, "enjoy your game."
My mother tried to give him a few bucks, but he refused.
"It was no trouble at all," he said.
And with that he walked across the aisle to the adjacent section,
found a patch of empty seats, chose one and sat down alone.
He did return, however, when the game ended for our reverse commute.
I imagine the grass was as splendidly green that day
as it has been in every major league ballpark I have visited since.
I imagine the crack of the bat and the roars of the crowd
thrilled me and drew me in permanently.
I imagine I stood halfway through the seventh inning
and sang "Take Me Out to the Ball Game" and smiled while doing it.
I imagine I either cheered a win by the home team,
or groaned with the final out of a loss.
I *imagine* all these things because, truth be told,   (cont)

I don't actually *remember* anything about the game itself,
but *everything* about a large black bus driver
who put me on his shoulders.
And how that one act of kindness
has informed how I see a portion of the world ever since.

Boulhosa

RUDE AWAKENING

Softly she snores her baby snores with the relentless
beep, beep, beep of the machine just 18 inches from her head.
She stirs only slightly when the door opens.
Bespectacled, he wears a white lab coat,
carries a small plastic basket and paperwork.
These are all bad signs.
It's 2:00 a.m., yet he speaks in a 2:00 p.m. voice.
"Maggie?" he asks, and though I whisper, "Yes,"
he fumbles with her wristband to confirm.
"I need to draw blood," he blurts out as he
turns on the bright light above her.
I see her squinting eyes fill with tears.
I have to be strong for her, I tell myself.
I am her daddy.
As requested I again pin down her legs, chest and left arm.
She wails the petrified wail that I now know well,
but will never get used to.
Her veins, like her, are tiny and tired,
and so it takes far longer than it should.
Then, in the moment I dread, our eyes meet,
and hers again ask mine*, Why do you let this happen?*
Aren't you my daddy?
I turn away and wait for it to be over, then softly kiss her head
and whisper in her ear, "All done, brave girl,"
as the gauze is taped to her arm.
Relieved, she manages a wave as he leaves.
The light goes off and I hold her for only a short time
before, spent from the trauma, she drifts back to sleep.
I know that it will take me far longer, as I stand beside her crib,
and listen to her snore her baby snores as tears roll down my face.
I am her daddy.

Boulhosa

JAN SHOEMAKER
THROUGH THE TREES

"You can't take things from a *grave*, Mom." My teenage daughters were bringing down the gavel as I plucked a sheet of paper from Thoreau's grave where it had been pinned under a pebble amid the offerings of pilgrims. Placed on top of the small, upright stone in the Thoreau family plot that read only "Henry," rather than among the coins and pens and flowers scattered more broadly, it had caught my eye.

"Watch me," I said, backing under a big pine where, unrepentantly, I opened the creased page to a poem and slowly read the half-dozen stanzas scrawled in longhand.

"Did you hear the planes fly over?" it began. This was July of 2002—the first summer following 9/11, and it quickly became clear that Corinne H. Smith, whose name was signed at the bottom of the page, had brought her bewilderment and sorrow to Concord's sages who are buried near one another in Sleepy Hollow Cemetery. "Did Concord's best decipher all the meanings of that act?" she asked. "Did Waldo make pronouncements?...Did Bronson take the other side?...And what about the voices of the women on the hill?" Nearby, the graves of Louisa May Alcott, Elizabeth Peabody, and Thoreau's passionately abolitionist mother, Cynthia Dunbar Thoreau, bore their own bounty in offerings. "Did you honor their opinions? Does the air carry them still?" Reasoning that one good rain would be the end of it, I refolded the poem and put it in my pocket.

Back home in Michigan the following week, I slipped the poem inside a frame and hung it on a wall in my high school classroom. Its handful of stanzas—so earnest and bemused, in the way of that disoriented summer—would usher my students into our study of transcendentalism in the following years as, for its part, the world steadily became more complicated. And as complication goes with being sixteen like breathing goes with air, it was a natural fit.

Sixteen, I'm noticing more than ever, is seriously young—younger than most of my clothes, half the age—give or take—of my own daughters these days. All of my students are post-9/11 babies. I feel the distance between us as I never did before. Last fall one of the Zoes in my 2nd hour showed me an app that matched selfies to classic works of art. "See," she said, offering me her phone. "I'm the Lady of Shalott." I downloaded the app and submitted my own picture. "Old Woman

Cooking an Egg," it said.

On the last day of summer this past year, I sat on a broad, flat rock in my garden among the hostas that overlook the lawn like consumptives, all lavender-gray and fading fast. Teaching, itself, was beginning to feel like a young person's game, most pointedly in its emphasis on the shiny stream of technologies that seem to hatch daily from the genius of small gods working off stage. It was hard to keep up. It was hard to *almost* keep up.

A few days earlier, during my school's open house a parent in the back row, sitting below a string of Tibetan prayer flags, called up, "And what technology do you use in class?" I had to admit that I didn't use much. I certainly don't arrange a platform for my students to chat up Hester Prynne online from their bedrooms. "Technology is great where it's needed," I answered, "like for distance learning, when students don't have the benefit of discussing ideas with people in the same room." I heard the pedantic tin in my tone, felt the rush of wind as I launched into a diatribe. "But we are living, beating hearts and minds who do convene in a room together—and what a rich and lively experience that is!" Those were all the cards I laid on the table—for the most part, they're the only cards I ever have. Like the words stamped onto the prayer flags that were rustling near the air-conditioner, I hoped my students' thoughts, generated by our reading and refined by our spirited give-and-take analysis, would lift and take flight.

Draped in a sheet on an examining table a few weeks earlier, I listened as my good doctor—a woman my own age—said, "There are three doors a woman walks through in life." We were talking about aging and the changing workplace. "The first leads to preparation—you're a student. The second door leads to a career and, for most of us, motherhood, and that long period where you give yourself to your job and family. The third door is menopause. After menopause, a woman's *only* job is to speak the truth."

Alone again in the examining room, I thought about truth-speaking as I put my clothes back on, about how aging can make us doubt our own conclusions—am I correct or merely a curmudgeon in a world that has rightly, naturally moved on?—and the extent to which our views will be valued. And I considered (again) the "professional" lines I sometimes cross in class when the current president puts out some barbarous new lie or blast of hate. Politically, teachers are supposed to remain neutral in class, which is to say, opaque as those eyeless old statues overlooking the atrocities of the Colosseum. But lately I'd been too often too outraged for silence, which felt like complicity, and I'd found myself making pointed remarks in our class discussions—most recently regarding "men who boast about building walls while having so few personal boundaries they brag about grabbing women's genitals." Gamely, I scrawled *HYPOCRISY* on the board, then asked, "What does *this* mean?" Almost daily, my mind drifted to the authoritarian rise of the Third Reich and I wondered how teachers in Germany had felt during the thirties. Did horrified Weimar democrats censor themselves among the ranks of true believers when their country made that murderous right turn that led straight to dictatorship and genocide? And weren't terms like "professionalism" and "neutrality" just uniforms we donned to take the heat off our squeamish moral responsibilities? And, day after day, I wondered if I might be getting too angry to teach.

Schlepping on my coat, I exited the examining room, turned the wrong way, as I always do, and let someone direct me to the parking lot. The next day I flew to New Hampshire, rented a car, and drove south to Concord, Massachusetts. Sixteen years after swiping a poem from Thoreau's grave, I was returning to the scene of the crime.

The Walden Woods Project, in its own words, "preserves the land, literature, and legacy of Henry David Thoreau to foster an ethic of environmental stewardship and social responsibility." As a part of this mission, twenty or so teachers from around the U.S. are invited to convene for a week each summer at the headquarters of the Thoreau Institute on a wooded slope overlooking Walden Pond. On the morning of our first day, I drove into busy, bucolic Concord and met the five other teachers with whom I'd be sharing digs, all of us introducing ourselves as we hauled bags up the old, steep steps of a cottage in town. Then we squeezed into my car and wove the winding few miles to Walden Woods to meet our larger group and push chairs into a circle in the manor house that serves as headquarters for the Institute. Paneled wood walls rose up around us and shelves at both ends of the room were thick with books.

We were young and old, from both coasts and the middle of the country. One of us had ridden horses in rodeos. Two had driven from Texas, camping in the rain with their indispensable third, a stolid bottle of Jim Beam. One of us was a novelist. One of us was pregnant with a child that we would all insist, as the week wore on and we got comfortable together, she name *Henry*.

"This was Thoreau's bean field, "our trail guide Brian, an

environmentalist from Brandeis, announced as our single-file group accordioned in around him where the path in the woods broadened. A few days into our week, we were just uphill from Thoreau's pond, the deepest freshwater lake in Massachusetts. Every summer morning, quite a few swimmers bisect it, most of them with flotation "bubbles" bobbing over their backs.

"All trees now," someone murmured. In Thoreau's day, much of the forest had been cleared to feed Boston's stoves and he'd planted and tended, not very successfully, a small crop of beans.

"None of these trees are more than eighty years old." Brian told us, "It's mostly pitch pine and oak." As we jotted field notes, he added, "Animals ate a tenth of his crop; Thoreau said it was a kind of tithe." I pulled a cluster or "fascicle" of pine needles from a sapling; its three needles told me it was pitch pine; red pines have only two needles per bundle, white pines five, we were learning.

We moved on through the woods, over a landscape that rose and dipped among geological kettles—basins left behind by stranded icebergs that had slowly melted away. "Henry used to drink here," Matt, our resident naturalist, remarked, pointing to a spring fringed by ferns and mossy boulders. I was noticing how often the staff referred to Thoreau as *Henry*—a friend. More noticeable was the way they pronounced his name:: *thorough,* as in, *a thorough explanation,* which was what, secretly, we were all waiting for regarding that jarring inflection.

"Yes," we were told when one of us finally asked. "Thoreau is rightly pronounced *thorough;* that's how Henry said it." I imagined taking that insider's scoop back to the Midwest—back to anywhere, really—and saw at once how *thoroughly* it couldn't be exported. You can't return from a week in London and start taking the *lift* or grow up sticking a fistful of dandelions in a *vace* and show up at a family dinner twenty years later with lilacs in a *vahz.* I stashed *thorough* away among the other mementos I'd haul home, most of them rocks dug out of the pond.

Sitting in loose rings around a big conference table in the library at the Thoreau Institute, we began our days with Jeff, who curates the manuscript collections at Walden, and Whitney, whose vision and grit organized our days and corralled us through them. We'd read all of the same materials sent to us in a syllabus the previous spring but I, at least, had never dug into Thoreau's journals, never read the entry where he describes encountering God in his own root cellar. "How many communications may we not lose through inattention?" he asks.

When Jeff brought out some of the Institute's actual manuscripts for us to hold, we lined up like novitiates and received the pages—Thoreau's slanted goose quill scrawl running over them—with awe. "One hundred and sixty-four Bibles:" Jeff said, "that's the length of Thoreau's journals."

Our afternoons were spent hiking and swimming and gliding in canoes along the serene Concord River where lawns roll down to the water from enormous, gabled homes. There's a lot of money in Concord these days. "Fuh-kin' gaw-geous is what we call this in Massachusetts!" Patty, who'd grown up nearby, called from her seat in the middle of a canoe Cindy-from-Missouri and I were paddling.

But lovely as our Walden days were, we carried the desperation of the times with us and everyone seemed to have descended on Walden Woods with the same visceral fear and loathing of the demolition machine that had been threatening to clear-cut the institutions of our democracy for the past couple of years. Would razed institutions simply grow back like trees? And what was our classroom role? No one was sure. By the time he wrote *Civil Disobedience,* Thoreau's own school had long been closed. But the transcendentalists' days had been fraught too, the future of *their* democracy threatened by the question of abolition: the *question*. There was nothing new about rampant American wrong-headedness.

Back in my classroom in Michigan, I thumb-tacked a map of the United States, the words: *America is Sacred: No Lies!* running across it at a diagonal, and thought about Thoreau's habitual, impolitic truth-talking. Then, on the first morning of class, when we all rose to recite *The Pledge of Allegiance,* I concluded my own pledge with a resounding, "with liberty and justice for *all races, all religions, all genders*!" and—big finish: "because this is America!" My students, startled at first, moved on to smiling and rolling their eyes, then to just eye-rolling, and finally to ignoring me altogether while they scrolled on their phones as I laid it out there day after day.

During the third week of school, I asked them, "Will Americans support national leaders who are bullies? Egomaniacs who rant and lie? Shameless power-grabbers who exploit people's fears while pretending to be patriots?" Eyes blinked in the little gulf of uneasy silence that followed. Then I threw a picture of Joe McCarthy on the *Smartboard* screen in preparation for reading *The Crucible* and we examined the way McCarthy lost the support of the American people once his character and abuses were fully known. "What *are* the obligations of citizenship?" I asked. "When do we say *enough?* We'll think about that for the rest of the year." Oblique or transparent, it's a question that has to be asked.. And after a week at Walden Pond, I have good reason to believe that teachers across the country are feeling their way forward, no two in the same way, asking, asking, asking.

Concord was busy the day I drove in from New Hampshire and parked in the driveway of a white, columned church shouldering an enormous steeple, in the way of old Puritan meeting houses. As the door was open, I wandered into the vestibule and was greeted by a couple of friendly twenty-somethings sitting at a card table. "What's happening inside?" I asked.

"The Thoreau Society is having its annual meeting," the young woman replied as a question formed in my mind. "You don't—by any chance—know a Thoreau-loving poet named Corinne H. Smith, do you?" It was a ridiculous long-shot.

"I do," she answered and joined me at the small window where we squinted into the sanctuary at the backs of a hundred or so people spread throughout the pews. From the high pulpit in front, a genial-looking man with a stand of white hair was speaking. "She's there, in the middle, in the white shirt." My eyes settled on the back of a gray-haired woman sitting next to the center board that bisected the pews into equal segments. I eased open the door and slipped inside.

Halfway up the left aisle, I lit on the end of the plank I was suddenly sharing with the woman whose purloined poem hung on my classroom wall. As the Chair of *The Committee on Selections of Officers* replaced the society's president at the lectern, I began my slow slide along the empty-on-my-side pew. On each side of the pulpit, black-eyed Susans and Queen Anne's lace in old jugs stirred in the small wind of oscillating fans. "One hundred and eight people voted in our election," the Chair reported, pausing: "with no evidence of Russian involvement." A light laughter rippled through the pews as, inch by inch, I bore down on Corinne. When I reached the bisecting plank that separated us like an old Yankee bundling board, a man to our left rose to address the acrimony between members of the Thoreau Society and members of the Emerson Society. Polarization was clearly everywhere.

Snaking my arm up the side of the partition in our pew, I passed Corinne a note on a page torn from my journal and watched her give it a quick scan. "I am Jan Shoemaker," it said. "I took your poem from Thoreau's grave 16 years ago." At the moment she turned to look at me, I like to think a bit of transcendentalist awe opened in us both.

Later that week, Corinne showed me around town, pointing out the stone marker where Thoreau's infamous jail cell once squatted, the saltbox house he died in (up for sale for a couple of million bucks), the busts of Concord's luminaries in the Free Public Library. Among them, Bronson Alcott's famous daughter Louisa's looked down from its pedestal. Despite reprisals threatened by the Fugitive Slave Law, that murderous legislation enacted by the governing scoundrels of their day, the Alcotts had made their home a stop along the Underground Railroad.

In the transcendentalists' divided nation, it took a war to dismantle the scabrous institution of slavery which, as newly free African Americans made economic and political strides, was replaced by Jim Crow. Even my current students, with their handful of years, can recall the times before gay men and women could marry. I am old enough to remember a family story, whispered at my aunt's kitchen table, of the afternoon, before R v. Wade, when my cousin limped, bleeding, off a Greyhound bus she'd secretly taken to and back home from Mexico. "What is once well done is done forever," Thoreau maintained, mistakenly. Even in its errors, Concord seemed to emphasize the way we inch forward and slide back, inch forward and slide back. Apparently, hard-won human rights are never *fait accomplis* and vigilance is not something we can afford to let slide. It seems that only by paying attention, by keeping about us a bit of the root cellar, can we hold a higher ground.

Naturally, during my week in Walden Woods, I revisited Sleepy Hollow—you don't go to Concord without stopping by to see *Henry*. The usual trinkets littered his grave—but no poems. At the cairn of boulders that marks the site of his cabin, however, I found another sheet of notebook paper with a message scrawled sloppily by someone bent over a knee.

"I know of no method or discipline that can supersede the necessity of being ever on the alert," it read. "HDT"—then, "Thank you Henry."

"Thank you, Henry," I echoed. And, in keeping with that old wisdom about paper covering rock, I replaced the note where I'd found it and walked down to the pond.

MEREDITH DAVIES HADAWAY
OCTOBER: THE WEEK IN REVIEW

A seal slapped a kayaker in the face with
an octopus.

An occurrence—he said / she said / said
the octogenarians.

A musical interval, but also the first eight
lines of a sonnet.

Speaking of music, does anyone really
play the ocarina?

October is *not* the eighth month of the year.

Occasionally, I wonder about these things.

VIGIL

>What if she outlives me?
>Me—trundling through my
>
>day with its careful "to-do"
>list. The old cat strutting from
>
>food bowl to spigot on little
>matchstick legs that could
>
>ignite at any moment, pausing
>to pee whenever, wherever
>
>she feels the urge. I bow to my
>feline queen and rise to turn
>
>the knob of the faucet. *Let our
>lives flow on,* I say, adjusting
>
>>the stream to a trickle.

Hadaway

STEVEN BEAUCHAMP
TYBEE REVISITED

Walking along the beach, I feel as if
I'm on a sidewalk between the gently rolling surf
and a downtown business district
with hotels, motels, condos, painted in varying shades
of yellow, pink, and beige, crammed
into every square inch of beachfront.
Concrete and wooden decks loll out of every building
like huge ramps from moving vans,
small swimming pools in between.
In season, vacationers walk, run, jump,
splash, eat, drink, dance, ride bicycles.
Pop music blares from bars and clubs.

Between the pools and decks, small mounds of sand
sprout like warts, sparse sea oats swaying in the breeze,
morning glory vines wreathing their borders.
These vestigial remains of sand dunes take me back
to an early photograph my mother took
on this very same beach years ago
with her Brownie Hawkeye in black and white.
She stood between the surf and me
and snapped the shot while I in cotton diapers
crawled toward her and the sun.
My head is erect, back straight, eyes wide and shining,
as I clambered like an albino baby sea turtle
toward the salty, all-mothering surge of the sea.
Behind me sand dunes rise and fill the backdrop,
bristling with sea oats, palmetto fans, and vines—
no stores, no houses, no hotels.
In the distance one lone telephone pole, slightly crooked,
adds the only vertical and horizontal lines
in a world of gently curving sand and fractal clouds.

They seem to me now like images from another world,
something made up for the closing scene
of an episode of *The Twilight Zone*.
Sometimes I wish they had never existed
so now they could not be so utterly gone.

TESSA SMITH MCGOVERN
FOR BETTER OR FOR WORSE

For better or for worse, your wife always says. You can hear her saying it now, her words loud in your ears. You smile. You see her face with red-apple cheeks and flyaway gray hair and that look of fake exasperation on her face, and you think, *Lazybones, get up and find her!* She must be downstairs in the kitchen already, in her pink dressing gown and worn sheepskin slippers, making tea.

You open your eyes and see the iron rail at the end of the hospital bed. You close your eyes again. Her face, the words, for better or worse, echo and fade. You are not in pain. You are warm, lying flat, cocooned in a comfortable bed, and the light behind your eyelids is bright. Have you had an accident? You shift cautiously in the bed. Still no pain.

You hear women greet each other loudly. You open your eyes. They must be in the hallway. Beyond the two small tents of your feet, past the end of the white bed, is a plain white wall with a framed print of a faded, red rose. To your right, actual, real daffodils in full bloom, shockingly yellow, stand erect in a white vase on the windowsill.

Above them, taped to the glass, is a card with a child's drawing of a red stick figure and the words " I LOVE YOU, GRANDPA." Behind the card, gray clouds sit on green treetops. Further right, a drip snakes down from nowhere, taped to the white hairs of your forearm, running along your wrist and the back of your hand, and disappearing under a large Band-Aid.

A face appears above you. It's a woman in blue hospital scrubs holding a plastic tray. She peers down at you and, loudly, says, "Mr. Black? Mr. Joseph Black? Helloooo! How are you?"

You speak but hear no sound. Why does nothing come out? You cough and splutter, and in the coughing, you find you still have a voice.

"Where's Dora?" you croak.

She frowns and sets the tray on the bedside cabinet. "I am Helena."

Her accent is Eastern European, her hair is the color of...that vegetable, what is it? Tomato, no, something else. Purple.

She leans over you. Her eyes are heavily ringed with black eyeliner, and she has a small, silver ring in her nose. "Are you ready for deeenner?"

"Where's Dora?" You imagine her, moving slowly, getting the

box of sugar cubes and dropping two into your teacup, stirring the tea as she gazes out of the window at the rusty bird feeder on the patio.

Helena's thick black eyebrows pull together, and she presses her lips in a thin line, considering you for a moment. Her eyes soften. She pats your arm. "We have turkey and stuffing and some deeleecious gravy! Are you hungry?"

Oh, you think. *There is no downstairs in this place. No patio, no bird feeder.*

"With mashed potatoes! You like that."

Eggplant, you think. *That's the name of it. Helena's hair is the color of eggplant.*

JOHN KRUMBERGER
SPILLED MILK

No use crying over spilled milk
—a phrase used often in that age
when milkmen still delivered
to houses on Franklin, not yet razed,
and Mr. Dresen's Great Dane 'Laddie'
—actually gentle as a lamb-
leaping, one perfect summer morning
clear over a back yard fence
and the approaching deliveryman
converged at the back door
the exact same moment,
the way the orbit of moon and earth
might sync together
once every half-millennium;
and the poor man shrieked,
and milk of course was lost;
my father the only witness
recounting it as best he could
while laughing so hard
that tears streamed down his cheeks.

ARTHUR GINSBERG
ON A PERSPECTIVE OF THINGS

Everything hinges on belief in the invisible.
Faith follows from this. The suspension of belief
may result in obsession with only the shining surface,
and skew one's life in the mode of shallow thinking.

When the moon obscures the sun, the lovely corona
of rays that escape around the edges, that slight bend
of light proved one man's vision of time and space.

Curiosity for the hidden may seem trivial compared
to the mouth-feel of caramel chocolate, or milk
of the galaxy spread across a darkened sky. Granted,
those modest pleasures are gifts given through tongue
and eye, a foil for what lives deeper inside, if one has
temerity to gaze through a magnifying lens.

Lucretius, a visionary of audacious courage, mocked
by pagan Rome, surmised long before quantum theory,
we came from particles spawned in a time of chaos,
free will depends on the capricious swerve of atoms,
the body, the vessel that holds mind and spirit.

I am riveted by the beautiful mystery, as he was,
even as I struggle with God.

From my home, I can hear shore birds singing
from their nests on the beach, invisible waves that spiral
into my ears. And, intricate spider webs studded
with jeweled raindrops, lure winged travelers.

Most rapturous of perfections is the jiggle of atoms
through the brain, to summon your mind like a monarch,
and command your thoughts,

to secretly lift the veils.

THE BONES ARE SINGING

At Dover Air Force base, the Corporal
bends to his work with the focus
of a diamond cutter, drapes the bones

in the Stars & Stripes, pins the Purple Heart
to the casket's satin lining. Bleached bones
that were interred in a rice paddy,

found glinting beneath the starlight
of a summer's night, come home now after
thirty years, to a daughter not yet born,

when her father was called to war. Leg bones
that carried him into battle, arm bones
that would have cradled her, the perfect

tongue & groove joinery of his spine, scaffold
for the flesh, still straight and unyielding.
She arrives to honor him, the last and only time

she will meet her father. In what seems
an audacious act of grief, she curls her hand
around his vertebrae—adoration rising

from the macabre—begins to hum a lullaby
under her breath. Reconstructs in her imagination,
the man from these hallowed bones, the father

she knows only from yellowed photographs,
clad in camouflage, beside a helicopter. The note
found in his foot locker promising her to come home.

And everywhere, in far flung fields & forests,
beneath glaciers and deserts, ancient & contemporary,
the orphaned bones are singing…

Ginsberg

ELECTION

An incessant ringing of chimes
as autumn sweeps summer's festering bounty,
and the honks of geese, loud, thumping wings
glide into our meadow for a fallen apple feast.

They do not know of ballot boxes
or man's petty bickering but follow
their own compass, as a vessel on auto-pilot,
over muzzle-flash, mountains and corn fields.

They do what is right for their kind;
stay together for life, lay eggs in the spring,
nurture goslings. They are peaceful at my table,
waddle softly through the fleshy, red-skinned fruit,
drape wings over each other by the shore,
to settle for the night. At dawn, in a thick fog

I hear their clamor, like children rising from sleep,
see blurred brushstrokes of black and white
as they lift away for southern climes. A "gaggle"
better describes my kind, unkind in their pecking
and plucking like caged chickens, sullied nests,
and cracked eggs. Behold that royal entourage

high in the heavens, while we beat feeble wings,
pollute the airways, and cower behind desperate
migrations, smugly, self-satisfied as we ink out
little boxes on a sheet of contenders, and wait
for frenzied voyeurs of our misappropriations,
the morning after, to say, who will weep, and who
might save for us and them, the water and the sky.

Ginsberg

X-MAS HEART-STRING

When the horse could not breathe,
grandfather towed it with the tractor
away from the barn to the creek,
shot it in the head, left her there
for the coyotes and crows, the way
some monks are left for sky burial.

Told his three-year old grandson,
Bonnie had gone to a happy place
where all old creatures go to rest.
When the boy asked if he could visit,
his mother said he would always be
attached by a heart-string he could pull,
to let Bonnie know he remembered her,
the times she carried him on her back.

Later, the boy dreamt he would die,
asked if Dada would come to see him
and Bonnie in that place. His mother,
speechless, felt a great weight crush
her chest, fought back sobs. The boy
waited like the dog waiting to be fed.

When her throat unclenched, she said
he would not die until he was very old,
had many children and grandchildren
of his own, reminded him to pull
on the heart-string whenever he felt sad.

And you, my mother beneath the snow-
laden meadow, can you feel this poet pull
on the heart-string stretched so many miles?

Then they sat around the tree adorned
with lights and baubles, and opened gifts.

Ginsberg

PAUL C DALMAS
NEVER HELD A BASKETBALL

I'm a soft, lumbering kid who's never held a basketball, so I stand by the blacktop court and watch them run and yell and shoot. I admit to myself that it looks like fun. In 1957 I'm only eleven, so even approaching the paved playing field of Bayside Junior High is an act of daring. These boys are older, bigger, and alert to the subtle intricacies of a game requiring speed, agility and competitive cunning. They're from a neighborhood where they've grown up playing in streets, dodging cars and knowing the sting of falling on asphalt. I know nothing. I'm an uncoordinated schlub, a kid more at home with books than sports gear. In a year I'll be a seventh grader, a student at this school, but now I'm a child who needs courage even to move past the chain-link fence in this rough, unfamiliar neighborhood.

An adult, the coach in my mind, is in charge. His face is tan and expressionless, his hands huge, and he wears a sweatshirt. He's not at all like my dad in his tweed jacket, brown slacks and tie.

"Hey," the coach shouts in a voice that comes deep from his wide chest, "Wanna play?"

I hesitate. I'm not ready for this, I think. These guys know what they're doing.

"Come play. They need one more," he says, gesturing vaguely toward the players. "That team."

Do I see a smile on his face or a smirk? I'm not sure, but I enter the court and begin running back and forth with the others. The only rule I'm sure of is that the ball must go through the net. I'm smart enough to stay on the edge of things, to find out how this game works, to keep from making a fool of myself. For a few minutes I just run back and forth with my team and engage in some erratic shouting. Things go well, then a loose ball comes my way and in an instinctive and thoughtless impulse, I grab it. Suddenly I am the center of the game. Half the boys hoot for me to pass to them; the other half maneuvers to stay between me and the basket. I am paralyzed with indecision, so I hold the ball over my head and, following the only rule I know, launch it wildly toward the basket. I watch it bounce off the backboard, balance for an instant on the rim, then fall impossibly through the net.

I can't believe what I have done, and I can't believe that what I hear is not cheering, but shrieks and laughter from both teams.

"No, no, no! You idiot." the coach shouts, "That's the wrong basket!" Then he grimaces and mutters to himself: "What a *stupid* thing."

I stand mortified. This is what I get for straying into foreign territory. The laughter of the other boys subsides.

"Just get out of here!" the coach says. "You shoot at the wrong basket and you shoot like a girl." He stares at me in disbelief. "What a screw-up!"

I head to the gate in the chain-link fence. As I leave I turn back a last time and see words on the coach's sweatshirt: Bayside Junior High P.E. Department

. . .

Because its name evokes a place of shelter for pleasure boats, Bayside Junior High sounds like a refuge. It's located near mooring for a hundred sailboats and cabin cruisers with varnished teak and polished brass. But among my classmates at Lincoln Elementary, the school's reputation is terrifying. Like most of the students at my school, I'm a nice kid from a nice neighborhood who rides a two-wheeler to school and returns home to conscientiously complete my homework. While I sometimes force myself to tolerate my teacher's idiosyncrasies or moodiness, most of the time I am genuinely fond of her. Lincoln's recess yard is a cheerful expanse painted for hopscotch and circle games. While the more athletic kids play kickball at lunch, anything as organized as a team is a mystery to me. And games with bats or baskets are after-school endeavors for the cool and talented few.

Bayside Junior High, I hear, is a place where the boys shuffle about in jeans and white tee-shirts like young James Deans. They brag about smoking and know where to buy cigarettes. On their shoes they wear heavy horseshoe taps that rasp menacingly against the sidewalk. The girls wear tight sweaters and waist-defining skirts with slits that reveal glimpses of calves. They are reputed to know things I don't want to imagine. I hear rumors of bloody fights and of bullying ninth-grade hall monitors who send you to the principal if you run down the stairs or don't keep to the right as you walk between classes. The teachers are uniformly strict, enforcing a complex canon of rules about hall passes, attendance and tardiness. Strict penalties apply for the slightest infractions. The worst stories emanate from the P.E. department. The gym is the lair of teachers who aren't just strict; they hate kids. Worst of all is Mr. Gustavsen, a P.E. teacher whom I have never seen, but whose forbidding name has already penetrated the peace of my sixth-grade existence.

Craig Peterson is the boy in my class I absolutely want to be. He's a blue-eyed tow-head who charms teachers with his jokes, excels at mixed fractions and flirts with the prettiest girls.

It is June, just a week before summer vacation and just three months before seventh grade. For weeks my classmates and I have anticipated something our teacher calls Matriculation Orientation. On the appointed afternoon, we climb on busses and ride to Bayside Junior High for a half-day tour. "Just to be sure things go smoothly for everyone in September," our teacher tells us. Craig Peterson, as usual, is the savvy one who knows what to expect. "It'll just be a bunch of boring talk about rules," he says. I listen carefully. With two older brothers who attended Bayside, Craig has provided most of my unofficial knowledge about my future in junior high. I decide it's smart to stay close to him during the tour.

After an hour in the musty auditorium listening to the principal and the student body president tell us what a fine place Bayside is, we take a walking tour of the school. The place is huge: a three-story maze of gray hallways lined with lockers, strange-smelling science labs with mysterious equipment, and high-ceilinged shop classes with machines that can maim us, we are warned, or worse. The tour ends at the P.E. Department, where the girls are escorted away by a tall woman in sweats.

We boys sit on mats in the gymnasium. I squeeze in next to Craig, and he tolerates my sitting next to him. Into the gym strides the head of the P.E. department. His hand holds a long hardwood paddle, an instrument of punishment and instruction. I recognize the man's huge size, his deep voice, his tan face, and the impenetrable look on his face. This is the man who, months earlier, identified me as an idiot on his basketball court.

"If you stay to the rules," he announces, "you'll never find out what this paddle is for." He pauses for a moment and scans us slowly, making chilling eye contact with each of us. "I am Mr. Gustavsen," he continues. "That's Gustavsen with an *e,* not an *o.* I am not Mr. G., and I am absolutely not Coach." Again he pauses and scans us. "Any questions?"

There is silence, then astonishingly, a hand goes up next to me. Craig is about to ask something. He smiles impishly and says, "How about if we just call you Gus?"

Mr. Gustavsen cocks his head to one side, curious about this impetuous little rodent. Then his mouth twists and he reaches down to grab Craig by the arm. With a few quick steps Craig, Mr. Gustavsen and the paddle disappear out the gym door. Thirty boys gasp. I remember the dark rooms we have passed on the way to the gym but cannot imagine where Craig has been taken. A second P.E. teacher steps smoothly to the front and begins instructions about the gym clothes and tennis shoes we will need for class in the fall. Craig is not on the bus for the return trip to our school.

. . .

Thirty, eighteen, twenty.

It is fall and my first day in P.E. class. Among the worries that follow me, the greatest is that I will forget my locker combination. I concentrate on remembering it, so I don't think of all the other things that worry me.

The locker room is worse than the gym itself. It is a windowless place with long rows of small metal doors, each about a foot square, behind which I keep my new gym clothes and shoes. From the lockers hang cheap combination locks that are notorious for not working properly.

Thirty, eighteen, twenty.

On one wall a closed gray door separates us from the windowed coaches' office that overlooks us as we strip and change into our gym clothes. Somewhere in there is Mr. Gustavsen's paddle. The office is forbidden territory unless we are summoned over the P.A. that squawks from time to time above the din of young male voices. My locker is next to Balestreri's. He is a ninth-grader with no first name. He's just Balestreri and already a man: baritone voice, broad shoulders, thick arms, and body hair that is an unsettling reminder of the changes that will soon overtake my own smooth-skinned self. *Thirty, eighteen, twenty.* Amazingly, my lock releases. I undress and change quickly, facing the wall of lockers to maximize my privacy.

On this first day we are to learn the rules. I already know I should line up on my number. I am number twelve in the second row. A good location, I think. Close enough to see what's going on but not exposed. I stand with legs apart and arms behind my back, wearing only tee-shirt and shorts as the wind whips around me in the cold eight-a.m. air. Mr. Gustavsen arrives. He wears thick sweat pants, a sweat shirt and a woolen car coat.

"It's freezing!" he shouts, "and you little worms are the reason I'm out here."

I already know the rules—I've read them repeatedly in the student handbook—but it's time to learn them again.

"First off is never be tardy," says Mr. Gustavsen. "That don't just mean be here. And it don't just mean standing on your number. It means *covering* your number with your feet. He pauses to let it sink in. "If I can see your number, you're tardy and you run laps."

I move my feet slowly together to obscure my number twelve.

"Next is don't screw around during calisthenics." Again a pause. "Screw around and you run laps."

I'm not 100 percent sure what a calisthenic or a lap is.

Mr. Gustavsen continues: "Now your gym clothes. They always got to be clean. That means you take them home every Friday and your mother washes them. That don't mean you take them home without getting them washed. I'll check every Monday. There'll be a sniff test." He allows this crucial motivation to sink in. "And you don't just carry them off in a wad. You roll your shorts around your socks and your sweatshirt around your shorts. It all makes a bundle. Then you use two rubber bands around the roll, one at each end. A neat bundle. So don't forget your rubber bands. I'll be checking for that on Friday and Monday, too. No clean clothes and you run laps."

The rules go on. "Showers," he says. "You shower after every class and that don't mean you just dance through the showers. You get wet. You soap down everywhere—I mean everywhere. Then you rinse off." Again one of those pauses. "And only one towel. That's all you need, so just one." He thinks for a moment. "And Mr. Antonopoulos, the equipment manager. You obey him just like he's a teacher."

I've seen Mr. Antonopoulos. He is dark with a fringe of black hair around his bald head and a blurry tattoo on his forearm. His purpose in life seems to be to stand at the towel window next to the showers and enforce the one-towel rule. "Take more than one towel," Mr. Gustavsen concludes, "and you run laps."

Next come the rules for running laps, which I come to understand will mean exerting myself until my legs are weak and I gasp painfully for breath. "There's an exact route you run," Mr. Gustavsen says pointing. "You go past the softball diamond, along the back fence, then you turn left and go along the basketball courts and back here. No cutting corners. You cut corners and you run extra laps."

He thinks again, then: "One last thing. No ogling the females." The word puzzles me. The girl's class is across the field, where they stand in lines wearing shapeless, dark blue uniforms and, I assume, are hearing their own version of the rules. I try to imagine what ogling one of them would involve. "Miss Andretti don't want you staring at the females," Mr. Gustavsen clarifies, "so you ogle them and you run laps."

Class concludes with Athlete's Foot Inspection. Mr. Gustavsen points to a wooden chair he has brought from a classroom. He is about to determine if we are free of foot fungus. "You see that chair? I want you to take off your shoes and socks, then come up here one at a time. You put your foot on the chair and you spread your toes to show me you got no Athlete's Foot."

Inspection takes about thirty minutes and class is over. I walk back to the locker room, carefully keeping my eyes averted from the girls' side of the field. I work my locker combination—*thirty, eighteen, twenty.* I shower, observing the rinse-soap-rinse procedure, then dry with a single towel and head for my English class. I've made it through the first day.

. . .

Weeks pass. Each day my route to the locker room takes me past the door to the gymnasium, the door out of which my friend Craig disappeared months before. Sometimes I stop and peer inside. Everything is strange and intimidating: the high ceilings, the creaky wooden floors and the sweaty, acrid stink of the place. Thick ropes hang from rafters twenty feet high. One day, I think, I will be expected to climb one of those ropes. I know what the rings are, and I've seen older kids performing feats of agility and strength on them. In the corner is a device I have learned is called a horse, and when I look at the chin-up bar in the corner, I squeeze at my doughy biceps between my fingers and thumb.

One day as I pass the door, Mr. Gustavsen stands beside it leaning against the wall with his arms crossed. For the first time since that day on the basketball court over a year ago, he speaks to me directly.

"Wanna see what's going on in there?"

It would never occur to me to refuse anything he suggests, so I nod and he points a thumb at the window in the door. Through the circle of wire-mesh glass, I see two boys in their gym clothes, both wearing boxing gloves. They swing wildly at one another. Most of the blows don't land, but the taller boy is doing better. Every third or fourth swing smashes against the other boy's head making him stagger for a moment until he receives another blow.

"Those two little worms wanted to fight. So fine, they get to fight." He smirks. "Some kind of argument about an ink-pen. All I know's that I caught 'em wrestling in the locker room."

He glances through the window. The smaller boy is on his knees, but the taller one is still pounding at him. "They wanted to fight, so they get to fight. That's the way it works."

I've never been in a fight in my life, but I imagine myself in the place of the smaller boy. What, I think, does it feel like to be punched like that? My gut tightens.

"That's all there is to it," Mr. Gustavsen says. "They go at it till it's decided."

Decided, I think. What does it mean?

I remember the time. I don't want to be late to class, so I turn and run to the locker room. Somewhere behind me I hear Mr. Gustavsen's deep hoarse laugh.

. . .

A week later, I'm changing in the locker room. Over the shouting male voices, I think I hear my name from the ancient P.A. system that summons suspected rule-breakers to the coach's office. The device, decades old, is incapable of reproducing comprehensible human speech.

Balestreri, the scary ninth grader whose locker is next to mine, understands. "They want you, kid," he says. "Whaja do?"

I just tie my gym shoes and head for the office where I stand in front of the glass door until Mr. Gustavsen notices me.

"What ya want, Dalmas?" he says, reading the hand-lettered name on my sweatshirt.

"I heard my name on the P.A."

"Well, why'd we call you?"

"I don't know, Mr. Gustavsen."

He closes the door, leaving me outside. Among the coaches drinking coffee within, I hear muffled conversation that includes my name. Then the door opens.

"Nope, it's not Dalmas, it's Thomas. We want Thomas." He stares at me blankly for a moment. "Well, don't just stand there. Get to class. You're gonna be tardy."

I scurry back to my locker. Everyone has headed off to the field, but standing in front of my open locker door is Balestreri. In one hand he holds my pants; in the other he holds my wallet.

"What're you doing?" I say.

His response is a hard slap across my face. I move to rub the sting from my cheek, but he grabs the front of my sweatshirt and shoves me against the lockers. My head thuds against the metal door, and he holds me there, half off the floor with his face inches from mine. I'm terrified by the strength in his arms.

"Listen, you little turd," he spits through his teeth, "you say anything about this and I'll kill you. I'll find you after school and I'll beat you bloody."

I nod slowly, holding back tears.

"You got that? I'll kill you."

I nod again.

He bangs my head against the locker again, then releases me and is gone.

I slide down the lockers to the floor. My head spins and my heart drums in my chest, but I catch my breath and climb to my feet on wobbly legs. My wallet, empty of my lunch money, is on the floor next to my clothes. I throw them into my locker, slam the door and make my way outside.

At dinner that night, I tell my parents. My dad furrows his brow. "Just forget it," he says. "Steer clear of that kid." He pauses for a moment, then puts hand on my shoulder and adds: "And be glad you're not him."

. . .

Standard gear for all students is a three-ringed loose-leaf binder divided into sections by class. In it, each of us carries homework, notes, a supply of lined paper and a zippered plastic pouch for pencils, erasers and a ballpoint pen. Each of us has a binder, but the way of carrying it is gender-specific. A boy grabs his by the thick end and props the other against a hip at his belt. A girl clasps hers to her breast, almost like a shield.

One day I arrive for class early and stand next to Teddy West among the boys waiting outside for Mr. Gustavsen to open the locker-room door. Teddy looks even more out of place in a P.E. class than I do. He is a pale boy with thick blond hair, hollow eyes and a bad case of acne. He is thin, fragile even, with almost no chin. And he clutches his binder close to his chest.

Teddy stares into the distance and I follow his gaze across the asphalt to the line of girls also waiting for class. There are all kinds of girls: tall ones and short ones, skinny ones and heavy ones, blond- and brown- and red-haired ones, girls in full flouncy dresses and girls in tight slinky skirts.

"You like girls, West?" From the doorway behind us, Mr. Gustavsen has appeared and is looking directly at Teddy. "You like to look at girls? Well, that makes sense. You look like a girl—an ugly girl. You walk like a girl. And you carry your binder like a girl. Just like a girl."

Teddy, incapable of any other defense, drops his binder to his side.

"You like to look at girls so much. That's fine. You take a close look at them. I don't want you in my class today. Go over to Miss

Andretti's class. Go have class with the girls today. Just sashay right over there, then you can have a good look." Mr. Gustavsen pauses. "The rest of you worms get inside and change. You're gonna be late."

Ten minutes later I'm on my number as Mr. Gustavsen finishes taking roll.

"Look," he says pointing across the asphalt, "look over there at West."

I see Teddy next to the girls' volleyball court. He stands at the net, still in street clothes. His head hangs and his shoulders stoop forward. He angles his eyes and torso so that he avoids looking at either the girls playing near him or our male eyes in the distance. His binder lies at his feet.

. . .

Two different things: swats and paddling.

Swats are harmless. Sometimes on days when it suits his mood after we've played baseball or basketball, Mr. Gustavsen makes an announcement.

"Losers line up. Winners get swats."

I shuffle into a long row with my fellow losers.

"Winners, take your places."

And each winner takes a place behind a loser.

"Okay," Mr. Gustavsen says, "assume the position."

I bend over and grab my ankles, placing my butt high in the air.

"Let 'em have it," he orders.

With that, each winner winds up and takes a palm-open swat at his loser's rear end.

It hurts and I hate it, but mostly it's just humiliating; and during P.E. class, anyone with my lack of skill is accustomed to humiliation.

Paddling is more serious. Since that first day of class, when Mr. Gustavsen strode back and forth explaining the rules, I've never seen the paddle. From time to time, I hear rumors about the it, stories usually centering around flouting the rules or insulting a P.E. teacher, but I never see the thing itself. Still, the threat hangs over all of us. I imagine stinging pain and not being able to sit down.

After the incident with my wallet, I stay away from Balestreri. This isn't easy. I hurry to the locker room before he arrives each day and change, then run to the field. Still, when we do meet, a strange truce exists between us. It's as if keeping my mouth shut has placed us both in the same disreputable fraternity. I'm not a squealer, he seems to have decided. I'm not a rat. He thinks we share a code, but really I'm just scared.

Then one day I'm in the shower room, a dingy space with cold concrete walls, slimy floors and two dozen shower heads that spray water that is unpredictably scalding or freezing. I'm doing my usual quick rinse in a corner that affords some privacy. Balestreri appears and approaches me, hairy and muscular, but — I can't believe it — his eyes are filled with tears.

"That son of a bitch," he says. A man's words said with a boy's whine. "He whacked me like nobody ever got whacked before."

He turns and I see a fat glowing welt across his buttocks and I know it's the paddle from Mr. Gustavsen's office.

Balestreri steps into the shower, then as the hot water hits him from behind, he jumps out screeching a wild howl of pain.

He spreads his cheeks and twists to inspect himself.

"Look at me! Look what that bastard did to me!"

I see a thick stream of blood run from his crack and down his leg.

I am aghast. I turn away from him and walk without a word to the towel window. My tormentor is in pain, but I have no sense of redress or retribution. I just recall what my father told me: "Be glad you're not him."

. . .

This story has no elegant ending, no clear resolution, no moment of justice. I just get lucky. One day my father comes home from work and tells my mother and me that he's been transferred and we're moving. Within weeks I say good-bye to Bayside Junior High and find myself in a suburb of bright new homes where broad green lawns stretch under California sun. Young Jacaranda trees line the parkways, and the place seems to have only two seasons: warm and warmer.

Mr. Gustavsen, Balestreri, the ominous gymnasium and the dark locker room are in the past. At my new school I change clothes in a room with an unlimited supply of towels and high windows that admit dazzling light. The walls are golden and the lockers are bright red, the same colors as the short dresses in which pretty cheerleaders dance at pep rallies. My new P.E. teacher, whom everybody just calls Coach, knows my name. One day I pass him as I am finishing my daily lap, running hard but trailing my class. My lungs burn and I gasp for breath. He looks me straight in the eye. "Good run, Dalmas," he says.

I make new friends and begin to enjoy sports with them in afternoon pick-up games. I'm happy playing baseball in right field, a bucolic place where I'm seldom threatened by a fly ball that I will surely fail to catch. Eventually, I have a late growth spurt and become a six-footer who weighs 200 pounds. I am as clumsy as ever, but my friends are impressed with my size. Sometimes when we choose teams for football, I'm not picked last. I've grown big enough to knock other kids down and I enjoy it.

. . .

Years pass and a predilection that I develop for reading turns into a career. After college I teach English at a high school where students call their P.E. teachers Coach. Although I have little to do with school sports, some of those coaches are my friends.

In the afternoon I sometimes sit enjoying the peace of my empty classroom instead of grading essays. From beyond the window I can hear shouts from students practicing for after-school sports. The boys throw footballs in graceful arcs, and the girls play a game I don't understand that requires them to knock a ball across the grass with hooked wooden sticks. These youngsters are shouting encouragement to one another and thoroughly enjoying themselves.

For the first time in years, Mr. Gustavsen comes to mind. I think of him and of my own long-ago fears. As a boy, Mr. Gustavsen scared me; now he just baffles me. What did he think he was doing? My mind goes to the books I read and ask my students to read. Stories as different as *The Catcher in the Rye* and *Romeo and Juliet* describe mean-spirited adults who are oblivious to young people's fears. And I think of the really dark books I teach. *Heart of Darkness* and *Lord of the Flies* describe characters possessed by inexplicable viciousness.

I look again at the teens playing outside and shake my head. The day is over for them and they head home in boisterous, chattering clumps, but I'm still baffled. There's no explanation for Mr. Gustavsen. He was just mean. I think of my dad's advice about Balestreri and apply it to Mr. Gustavsen. I'm glad I'm not him.

ZACK ROGOW
GETTING PERSONAL

MERMAID seeks sailor for ongoing, part-time relationship. Must live near ocean. Discretion required. Wave blue hanky at sunset.

(cont)

SMALL IMP will mill straw into gold. Available for emergency hire, 24-7 service. Families with new firstborns only. P.O. Box 43095743.

GHOST brings back winter holiday memories. Volume-adjustable chains and armor. Low-maintenance, reasonable rates. Put "Spirit" in subject line so I know you're real.

FAIR MAIDEN needed to tame savage beast. Seeking animal lover, not afraid of long, sharp, twisty horn. Only responses with tapestry portraits will be answered.

MAGIC LAMP, 24K gold, includes genie. Priced to sell. Free shipping from Baghdad. Not responsible for results of wishes. Cash only, no returns.

CASTLE ROOMS AVAILABLE for children missing a parent. Must pay all costs. Will take good care of your child. www.wickedstepmother.com

KIDS' GETAWAY RENTAL IN ENCHANTED WOOD. Retro cottage with wood-burning oven. Travelers' insurance recommended. Don't even try bread crumbs.

PORRIDGE TASTINGS in secluded natural setting. Organic oats and homemade, local honey. Chairs and beds available at your own risk. Apply: Three Bears Realty, ask for "Doris."

FOUND: GLASS SLIPPER. If you left this at prince's ball last Saturday just after midnight, respond with shoe size. Please be single, DDF, and into LTR with royals.

Rogow

TO THE PERSON WHO HAD ME TICKETED FOR BLOCKING HIS DRIVEWAY

First of all I was *not* blocking your driveway
unless your personal vehicle happens to be as
wide as a Mardi Gras float
with the whole of Dixieland on top of it
and all I did was overlap a few fingers
of the red paint you slapped on the curb

to mark the area *beyond* your driveway
which just goes to show that your ego is so much
wider than your mind
and secondly your multimillion
glossy magazine Victorian
that you probably obtained through God-only-knows-what
scheme to pickpocket Mother Earth
proves there are millions of reasons
why you should find a productive way
to spend all your zeptoseconds
instead of phoning in tickets for the people
who circle endlessly around your neighborhood
hungry for a parking space
near the movie theater that constitutes the one and only
sign of life in the featureless void
that masquerades as your neighborhood
and lastly
please consider this poem
an invoice for $110
which is how much you cost me
but come to think of it
maybe you should be proud
maybe you in fact did something
to inspire another human being
for once in your life.

Rogow

HOLLY DAY
THE TREE IN OUR BACK YARD

She kneels on the ground beside me, and I put the tiny earpieces in her tiny ears
hold the silver disc of the stethoscope up to the peeling white bark of the river birch
press it firmly against the tree. I hold my breath and watch my daughter's eyes grow wide with delight
as she picks up the slow pulse of the sap moving through the tree, heavy and regular
as a heartbeat. "I hear it!" she whispers excitedly, reaches out with one hand

(cont)

to pat the tree as she would a large dog, or an elephant, or something magical from one of her delightfully incomprehensible dreams.

Once, her brother knelt beside me where I lay on my bed, this same stethoscope dangling from his own tiny ears, the silver disc pressed against my swollen belly. "I can hear her!" he whispered excitedly, finally, the pinch of worry gone from his face
as he felt his sister move. There are so many other things I could write about here of all of the days I waited to for the tiny fish wriggle of my daughter to come
but all that matters is that we are here now, by this tree. All that matters is this moment, right now.

Day

J F CONNOLLY
BAYONNE

On a Saturday morning in his senior year in high school, Carl's father was crushed to death. "Your father is hurt and can't drive home," his mother told him. He was cleaning the garage. "Deke called," she said. "He wants you to go get him and bring him home. I'll put clean sheets on his bed and make him lunch."

The port was fourteen miles from his house. The roads were open, and he drove as fast as his pickup truck could go. The late November sky spewed drops of rain on the windshield, and Carl worried about his mother. Recovering from another bout of pneumonia, she seemed weaker. His father had a way with her. He made her laugh. Carl was embarrassed that she looked so much older than the mothers of his friends, embarrassed that he felt self-conscious about her. She depended on his father for everything, and Carl knew that he should be more sympathetic toward her. Most days she sat in front of the living room window in her bathrobe like a made-up ghost looking out at the dapple willow trees in the front yard. As he pictured her in his mind, a low-rider with tinted glass swerved in front him, just missing the left fender of the truck. He realized that he was driving too fast and focused on the cars in front of him. He was a defensive driver and had never come close to an accident. There was no need to hurry because it was probably his father's knee again, the shrapnel from Vietnam. His father was strong, tougher than most of the men who worked for him. His father would be okay. He would be back to work in a couple of days because he carried on against anything that got in his way.

When Carl entered the terminal's parking lot, he saw Deke standing at the gate beneath the sign: *Military Ocean Terminal at Bayonne*. Deke was smoking and looking up at the gray sky and drizzle. Carl parked the truck in front of the gate, remembering how hard it had been for his father to quit smoking.

"I didn't want Ginny here," Deke said. He put his arm around Carl and pointed toward Pier 3. "I told her that your father asked you to come. I lied. You're old enough."

"Old enough for what?" Carl asked.

"Someone has to see what happened, son," Deke said. "And not your mother." He put his arm around Carl and walked Carl toward the docks. He told Carl that a Pacheco Crane was swinging a GVC Tank onto the ship that his father's crew was loading. His father, Deke said, walked under the crane when the crane snapped. "Just like that, out of nowhere," Deke said, "an 84-ton tank—it was like a bomb exploded."

Deke held Carl as he looked up at the broken crane dangling above them. Six feet from his father, Carl saw it—there was no body, just a red stain on the dock, the bits and pieces of what was once his father. He stared at specks of the flannel shirt his father wore, red plaid dots here and there, the yellow flecks from his safety helmet, his father's bones pancaked. There was no body. Carl fell to his knees and wept. Deke knelt down and held him. Carl leaned into Deke's chest, and mumbled, "Jesus, he's a crushed ant, Deke."

Two weeks after the funeral, Carl's Uncle Jack, asked Carl to help him carry his bags to his car. On the walkway, he said, "Ginny needs you —and Elizabeth too. You are the man of the house now. You have to take care of your mother and sister. You call me if you need anything." Carl knew that his uncle would not be much help. Uncle Jack lived on the other side of the country. He was retired and living on his social security checks, living as he said, "from week to week."

Sorrow owned Carl's house. He tried to snap his mother out of her silent grief, but she answered in a goblin-like nod or a one-word answer. When she was not at church, she sat in front of the bay window in the living room, her rosary beads wrapped around her fingers, her lips pursed and moving in a twitch. He thought that she looked like a mannequin that had come to life in a storefront window. There were bills to pay and the insurance company still had not sent the money. He was sure that the money would come soon, but he felt as if he did not know what he was doing when he was on the telephone talking to the people who had the money. He did not understand the two checking accounts, and his mother was no help to him.

He had missed two weeks of school and had work to make up. School could wait. His first foray back into the world of living was at the Y. He wanted to lift weights, to get back to a normal routine. As he was finishing his last set of bench presses, he stood up from the bench and heard a voice behind him.

"I know you. You were the football co-captain—right?"

He turned around. A short girl was standing in front of him.

"I'm Martha, but everyone calls me Marty."

He nodded to her. Her nose looked as if it had been broken. Rope-like veins laced her bicep muscles. "I've seen you around, in the corridors," he said. "You're the new girl."

"Yup. Junior. We moved here last summer."

He looked around the weight room. No one was watching them.

"You don't know me. Why would you?" she asked.

He surveyed the room again, looking for that man.

"No one is watching us, silly. Janie, she's my friend, told me about what happened and I'm really—

"I have to go," he said. He straight-armed the distance between them and picked up his backpack, "Look," he said, "I'll see you around."

She curtseyed and smiled. "Sorry. Your father—I get it. I know Mary Desilet is your girlfriend, but, look, we could be friends. You know why? Because I like girls."

The corridor was filled in the loud laughter and talk that heralded the first day back to school after the winter vacation. He stood in front of his locker, waiting for Mary. She had twice cancelled dates during the vacation. The last time that he had seen her was Christmas Eve. Her house was teeming with relatives and joy, and he felt out of place, leaving her after she opened her Christmas present and kissed him. He regretted the gift, inexpensive earrings that he bought because they were on sale. He should have spent more money. He should have stayed with her longer.

She came into view, in front of her locker and chatting with her girlfriends. He studied her, waiting for her to make eye contact with him. They had been going steady since September, but she changed after the funeral—that Saturday afternoon that she came to his house, his mother sitting at the window, smoking, coughing, *The Way of the Word* on her lap. "God loves the rain," she said. Mary looked at him in an eyebrow-raised stare that embarrassed him. "Yes, Mrs. Navickus, I understand, " she whispered.

He was sure that she knew that he was watching her. Billy Johnson walked up to her. She giggled and put her hand on his shoulder. She had dated Billy throughout the junior year. She had an early acceptance to Bowdoin and Billy had one from Colby. Carl knew that it was a natural fit—two smart book people who were on the same track. Mary's family was from Manhattan—he was Jersey and she was money.

The bell rang, and he watched her walk to her AP English, her first class. She laughed loudly and waved goodbye to Johnson. He knew for certain that she would go back to Johnson by the end of the month. She was moving on. Johnson would be her prom date. This was the way it was. Some people had it easy in life. It was as if their lives were a happy ending movie that they were writing year in and year out.

When he left school, his friend Paul was waiting for him at the truck. "Hey, buddy, your old 150 is still trucking on. Hey, you haven't called—"

"Yeah, I know," Carl said. He put his palms in front of his chest. "*Mea culpa*. Sorry I didn't call you back. Belated congrats on Rutgers."

Paul smiled and hugged him. He asked questions about how Carl was doing with "the death and all." Paul talked about throwing touchdown passes next year for the Scarlet Knights. He asked Carl if he had heard from Rutgers, and Carl told him that he had withdrawn his application, that he was too small to play for the Knights. Maybe he would apply to a NEASC school next year. College was not in the cards now. He had to take care of his sister and mother. There were bills that needed to be paid and a seventy-five-thousand-dollar insurance problem to resolve. Paul nodded. He said, "Hey, you're smart and, my man, you can do whatever you put your mind to doing. You'll be fine. Off to practice. Stay loose, Carl."

Carl watched Paul walk across the parking lot to the field until he was out of sight. Carl stood in silence, breathing deeply. Life was definition, defining words, problems, and the way the world defined people: money, education, class. He was not going to college. He would be a working man. He would be his father. Mary and Paul were opening a door that locked in front of him. One plus one equaled two, a simple truth, the digits of dollars and cents a definition that told him who he was.

As he climbed into his truck, he felt as if a ghost had appeared. It was that man again. He couldn't move, caught in the site of that the hulking creep, the man's finger pointing at Carl like a pistol. The man was three parking spaces from Carl. He sat on the hood of a sedan. He was smiling. He pointed to the gray letters emboldened on his red sweatshirt: *Sic Semper Tyrannis*.

Six weeks had passed and graduation was looming. Carl had separated himself from his friends who graciously thought that he was still coping with what they called his "loss." At the dinner table he asked Lizzy about her day at school. She said that she had a ton of homework and was tired. She asked him if he would help her, and he said that he would after he helped their mother with the bills. He washed the dishes and put them in the strainer. He swept the floor, that man entering his mind again. The first time that he saw the man was in the shower at the Y. They were alone, naked and washing. The man's buttocks had a large propeller tattooed on each cheek. Above the propellers, a tiny tattoo read "Twin Screws." When the man turned toward him, he cupped his testicles and jiggled them. He was fat and bald, his arms and chest sprouting a tangled weed of hair. He stroked his Van Dyke beard and sneered. Carl fled from the shower. Soaking wet, he dressed as fast as he could and ran from the Y to his truck. He saw the man two more times at the Y. At the far end of the weight room, the man glared at Carl. It was as if the man were trying to send a message, and Carl, secure in the knowledge that he now showered at home, pretended that the man was not there. When the man disappeared, Carl thought that the man was probably in jail, a convict, an alcoholic and a dope fiend whose life was living in and out of a cell.

Her elbows on her desk and her head resting in her hands, his sister looked up at him and smiled. "Bills, huh?"
Carl sat down. "The check. These insurance folks squeeze you until the last minute. That's their S.O.P."
"Dad used to say S.O.P. I never really got it."
"Standard Operating Procedure," Carl said. "You follow the procedural rules of a task that has to be accomplished. So what's your S.O.P. tonight?"
"I have to write a critical essay on this poem, "Ode on a Grecian Urn." It's due tomorrow, and I should have started writing it a couple of days ago. It's a three-night assignment and has to be three to five pages. Mr. Florio likes the five-page ones. I can't get started because I just don't get the poem."

She gave the poem to him. He read it and looked up at her when he was finished. He could tell that she knew that he was baffled. "Read it again," she said, "slowly, line by line."

Some students, he thought, seemed to have all the answers to all the questions. He knew that Lizzy was smarter than he was. Mrs. Buckley, his ninth-grade teacher, doted on him. Helping him with his homework, Mrs. Buckley told him that his I.Q. test score was average. She said that people who try hard reap success. She knew his mother. They were in the Ladies Sodality at the church. She told him that his mother and father cared about the poor, that donating and raising money for the poor, she said, was a sign that Carl had been "raised to think of others before himself." She said that "overachievers are special folks." She was a tiny woman, a hunchback with her left leg shorter than her right leg. She was the best teacher whom Carl had ever had, an overachiever herself. When Glen Menowski asked her what the word buxom meant, she was embarrassed and his classmates giggled. Later that day, she cornered Menowski as he was entering the lavatory. She grabbed his ear and pushed him against the door. Menowski never challenged her again.

"I can't help you. Poetry has always confused me," Carl said.

Lizzy said that Mr. Florio repeatedly told her class that a reader has to understand the intentional ambiguity in literature because it lets the reader participate more fully in her existence. Carl wanted to tell her that life was intentionally vague. You couldn't get the answers until you were old unless, as his mother would say, God gave you every answer to every question. But he did not say a word because Lizzy rambled on about the poem, saying that she thought that the beauty in the poem was about art. "If something is beautiful," she said, "that means you can trust it. It is not a lie, and so much of everything is just lies all over the place. Jesus' words are true because He said beautiful words like the words in the poem."

"That sounds like momma talking," Carl said.

Lizzy frowned. "You miss him. I do too."

"Yeah, it hurts," he said. He wanted to say that it hurt more for him that it did for her because he was his father's favorite.

Lizzy said, "It hurts me too. I just don't show it the way you do. Dad wants you to stop moping around the house. He wants you to fix the fence, take care of momma, and fix her problems. He doesn't expect me to do that stuff. You've got to respect momma and her prayers."

"I don't mope," Carl snapped back at her. Immediately he was sorry that he had raised his voice. "I love her... I do."

Lizzy stood up and hugged him. She said that she was sorry and did not want to make him feel bad. He nodded, his eyes welling up. He stiffened his body and pulled back from her.

"You really have helped me," she said. "Just talking with you. I'm going to write about how making something beautiful lives on forever. Well something along those lines. I'll figure it out as I am writing it."

Carl smiled and turned around to leave the room. As he did, she said, "You know Martha Tinsley? She keeps asking me about you. She is nice enough—you know, the new girl. She knows about you and Mary. She asked me if you've found a new prom date. I think she wants to go with you."

He was restless and could not fall asleep. He had to do a better job with his mother, stop feeling angry at her incessant coughing and wheezing. He would call the insurance company when he came home from school. He would fix the problem. And now everyone knew about Mary breaking up with him. In a way that seemed odd to him, he felt relieved. She had ended it politely as he knew she would. The truth was that she was just a girl whom he had dated because you had to have a girl. And the truth was that the man had to be confronted—he, too, had to be fixed.

He finished his second rep of 100 incline sit-ups. HIs daily workouts had become an answer to the blood-stained dock. He was happy because the insurance check came in the morning mail and because his mother was beginning to come back to the living. She was walking in the morning with her church friends, no longer sneaking a cigarette, and speaking in coherent sentences. Her life was in God's hands and belief was working for her.

His sister and his mother called it "the accident." He remembered reading the Caesar play in the ninth grade, fate not being in the stars but in the people. If the crane broke thirty yards down the pier, his father would still be alive. Carl wished that he could have his mother's faith. In the morning, before his sister and he left for school, his mother cited *The Book of Job*. "Who are we," she asked, "to explain God's ways?" Carl knew that the crane broke because it broke.

He left the Y and ran four miles at the high school track, looking to see if the man was in the distance and watching him. As the early night's dusk rose in the sky, he drove the nearby streets to find the man.

He felt disappointed in the thought that the man was gone again, gone, perhaps, forever. He needed to find him. When he drove onto his driveway and parked his truck, he grabbed his cell phone and called the new girl.

    At first it was an impulse. He took Marty to see a movie at the theater and then for ice cream sundaes. They talked school gossip about teachers and students. She asked him about college, and he lied to her by saying that he might apply next year. She said that she wanted to go to Carnegie Mellon and major in English because she could be a "big fish in a little pond." She said that most of the students at Carnegie majored in engineering or math and the sciences. She would get more attention as an English major. She wanted to be a playwright. Her favorite play was *The Glass Menagerie*. When he drove her to her house, he walked her to the door and asked for second date.

    He was not attracted to her, but she was pleasant enough and something about her that made him want to be with her. After their second date, he walked her to her porch, and she asked to come inside to meet her parents. Her mother and father greeted him with their condolences. They went upstairs to their bedroom. Marty took two cans of soda from the refrigerator and brought him into the den.

    At first, she did most of the talking. She asked him what his favorite novel was, and he said that he liked "To Build a Fire." She smiled and said that it was a short story. She told him that she loved movies. Her father had just bought a new sixty-five-inch television. He should come to her house to watch films some night, perhaps for their next date. "I know we're not going steady or anything like that," she said, "but I love three films that I would like to watch with you." She named the films, *Before Sunrise*, before this, before that, and went on and on about the films.

    She talked about her family. She said that her father's company transferred her father to New Jersey. He was a C.P.A. She was an only child. Her mother had two miscarriages before she was born. She was a "late baby." Her mother and father were "the best ever." Eventually, he began to talk because she asked him questions about his family, and he told her everything—spoke to her in a way that he never had with anyone else. When he got to telling her about the man, she starred at him wide-eyed. He left out the sexual details because he was embarrassed. He called the man a "stalker," and she seemed to know what he meant.

    "I can't seem to get him out of my mind," Carl said. "When I run or lift or hit the heavy bag, I imagine knocking him to ground and beating the blood out of him."

Marty smiled and held his hand. "I think that you need to let go of stuff." She said, "Some things are best left and not engaged. Men feel as if they have to encounter. It's in their DNA and the way that they have been raised. You know—nature-nurture and all that. Women are different. Duh? Of course they are, but women tend to accept what life gives them. He's a sick man. You don't have to beat him up. Call the police. He's not a fight on the football field. Don't you see?"

"Yes." He nodded to her and grinned. "I need to give him up." He laughed and then collected himself. "You're right, of course—I don't really know why I let him get to me."

"The why doesn't matter," she said. "It's the how am I going to put him in the past that counts." She giggled. "Look at me—little miss philosopher."

When she walked him to porch, she said, "I like boys too, you know—I like everyone." He kissed her. He drove home happy, and he fell asleep thinking of her. She shined the dull spots inside of him, a temporary glow that stayed the certainty of an ordinary life. He would invite her to the senior prom. They would be friends for a while, and then they would move on in the different directions of their lives.

He walked his neighborhood, thinking and planning. Every day seemed to be a new decision. And when that man returned—because the man was in his dreams, hovering over him—he would crush the man in a barrage of punches, leaving that man's face in a bloody pulp of skin and bone. He would do with this thought for now, knowing, of course that Marty was right, that he would turn around and walk away from that man.

He walked past the high school and entered the cemetery. At the top of the hill he saw a burial in the distance. A minister was talking to an old man and woman. The man leaned on a cane that he held in his left hand; the woman held his right hand. There was only one car: a black limousine. The undertaker stood behind the old man and woman, his homburg in his hands. Carl remembered his father's funeral which had at least one hundred mourners at the graveside, some of the terminal's crew gangs weeping. If you die old, he thought, you die alone. Caesar had many mourners, and Caesar's friend had Caesar's back. Anthony told the crowd the way of the brutal world of men. Carl, too, felt alone. Mrs. Buckley lived alone. If she lived long enough, this is how she would die.

He walked home. A late afternoon shower was passing. Carl stood in his backyard, staring at the damp grass. The sky was an oyster gray, the clouds drifting northeast. He remembered the late January afternoon that he and his father cut wood for two hours and then carried the firewood to the wood rack at the back of the house. His father said, "You're strong, son—strong for a ten-year-old whippersnapper." It was as if his father were still alive, trying to tell him that he was too young for this to happen. He wanted to be strong. He flexed the muscles in his chest and arms. He wanted to be like his father, a man who loaded vessels in the winter, wearing only a sweater and a watch cap in a defiance of the cold. That afternoon, eight years ago, Carl's father said, "The warmth of the summer sun is nothing more than the dying sunlight of winter." Carl knew, now, what his father meant.

  He loved his mother but not enough. He knew that he had to love his mother as his father had loved her. His mother prayed for everything, and Carl promised himself to champion her prayers and belief. His father had been a dutiful man. He expected little from life. Carl promised himself that he would tell his mother how much he loved her—and continue to say that he loved her because he wished that he had had the time to tell his father how much he loved him. He would take the job that Deke offered him. A stevedore made decent money—a government job with benefits and security. His life would be loading ammunition and equipment. His sister would finish college and be successful. Then he would find a woman whom he would marry. They would be happy because she would be someone who expected little from life. He would fix the carburetor in his mother's car, replace the wheels on the lawn mower, scrape and paint the peeling clapboard, caulk the gutters, and reseal the driveway. He would rebuild the sagging shed and sculpture the overgrown trees and shrubs. His life was the simple truth, and he could live in the understanding that he would give his sister entrance into a life that was now beyond his reach, that he would shoulder the routine of work and provide for his family, and in the knowledge that, even though it was not there, he brought the body home.

DEBORAH FLEMING
CHEMISTRY POEM

"Write a paper about your favorite element," the chemistry professor said, and so the chemistry major chose carbon, and I thought she should be

(cont)

more imaginative, until she explained, "Because it bonds with so many elements"; the physiology major chose calcium, the biology major nitrogen, the psychology major sodium, the business major silver, the political science major uranium, the theater major mercury, the foreign languages major molybdenum because she was the only one who could pronounce it, the engineering major iron, the physics major cesium because he was the only one who knew what to do with it, the art major gold, and the philosophy major lead,

but I chose oxygen because of the blood-red spheres they use
in those tinker-toy models of molecules,
and because—as climbers know at the airless roof of the world,
and divers know in the ocean's eyeless dark,
and the dying know as they cling to the last particles of their lives—

every breath we draw is our transfiguration,
every day a kind of exalted burning,
like the stars.

Fleming

PROPHET

In a Bart station in San Francisco the ticket machine would not take my twenty, no one was around to ask for help, and darkness was descending.

Suddenly a young black man hovered at my elbow. "Change machine's at the other end of the track," he said. "This one don't take nothing bigger than a ten. I need fifty cent to get to a homeless shelter." His tee shirt was torn across his chest. I followed his dreadlocks and lilting step down the platform. "Put your twenty in there, and it will spit out four five-dollar bills. I need five dollar to get to a homeless shelter." I did as he told, a slot just big enough swallowed my twenty, and four five-dollar bills descended into my grasp. I handed a five into his extended palm, whereupon he turned and disappeared into shadow.

At once the station master loomed before me, fortyish, white, clean, saying, "It doesn't help us when you do things like that." The young black man may have used the money to lose himself in the fog of drugs, for all I know. What I do know is that he gave me direction before the train burst out of the tunnel into the light to carry me to another world.

Fleming

AARON PARKER
LIVE A CIDE

why would you leave this
earth this way
don't you want us to listen
to what you have to say
when chance is given
you have to take a chance
apply it to your life so that
you can enhance
all that you are to let us know
what is truly your feelings
these things you have to let them go
but still let them show
you may think that your
life is worthless
but anything can be cleaned up
even what you call a mess
taking your life is never the answer
let's leave that to accidents
murder, and well, cancer

ROBERT GRANADER
CURABLE

I don't fear dying. Or at least not the way others do.
    I don't worry about missing my daughter's wedding or holding my grandchildren. I can see the next decade of empty-nest-hood as days piled on top of weeks trying to fill the empty hours I'd accumulated over the years like paid time off hours from work.
    I see the next decade as a time when my son will marry some woman my wife will hate, a daughter who will find pleasure in her work and not a family until it's too late, a wife who will sag with age.
    And for me? A continuing battle with the waistline, the hairline, the lines in my face that seem to arrive overnight and then fade

throughout the day, or really it's just my eyesight.

And so if the end should come, I won't fight it. I'm not one of those who wants to live to 120 and will fly to Denmark for some experimental treatment so I can stretch a six-month life sentence into seven months or ten or a year.

I only worry about the pain.

"Will it hurt?" is the first question I ask every doctor or dentist about every procedure and prodding. I hate physical pain because I can't run from it. Emotional pain is avoidable.

"I have been close to death," I told my therapist. "Not that I've almost died, but I feel close to it. Thinking of it, trying to grasp it."

"You have been acquainted with the night?" my therapist said.

"Ennui," I told him halfway through my 450-dollar hour.

"Ennui?" he said in a tone that made it sound like a question.

"Boredom," I said this time, expecting him to know everything from Freud to Strunk and White. "That is my affliction."

"I know what it means," he said.

"You didn't seem to," I told him, still annoyed that we started the session three minutes late. Sometimes that married or soon-to-be not married couple who has the time before me goes over their allotted fifty minutes and knocks me back a few. But I never go over. I leave on time either because I start to gather my things with a couple of minutes to go, or because he abruptly says, "See you next week," whether I'm in the middle of a sentence or a break in thought.

He thinks my problems aren't as severe as the married couple before me or the sad sack guy after me. The guy who lost a wife, I think. I don't know why I think that, but he looks lonely, doesn't wear a wedding ring, but dresses nice, like a lawyer about to see clients.

Since my problems aren't money or health, I'm not going broke or dying, it seems less dramatic or serious to him? There's nothing he's doing to make me feel this way, he would say, but I get this sense by the way he sometimes looks out the window like he's thinking, but he's just bored. Or the way he lets the couple ooze into my time. I shouldn't feel like I have to entertain him.

"There is a distinct lack of newness in this life of mine," I told him, "in case you hadn't heard."

"You've mentioned it," he said in his usual drone. "More and more since Nathan left for school."

Sometimes during therapy when I find that I have spoken about the same topic for too long, I tend to make a change. Not because I am over it or I'm getting better or solved it in some way where he can take credit, but just the boredom of it. Or maybe I get embarrassed about the continuing spiral of emotions built on my sinking ship of privilege and ease.

That's really not how I feel my life to be, but that's what he is thinking, doctor know-it-all, doctor judgment, doctor sit there and let me answer my own questions.

I know that from his chair, behind his baggy shirt and ill-fitting pants, horrible instant coffee and a belly full of breakfast bars, he is judging me and writing in his journal or telling himself that I am a spoiled middle-aged man with typical middle-aged man problems and he could be helping some suicidal kid or grieving widow if it wasn't for my time slot, but the truth is not many people would pay his price. So he needs me.

I can't stand his judgment, though he tells me it is getting in the way of my therapy, hindering my chance at success. But really, what is success?

Later that night the taillights came at me like red Tasers, boring holes in my eyes. The rain was pouring as my car farted along through Washington traffic. These people can't drive in the rain. In Washington, the level of bad driving is one notch above, or below, the rest of the world. Here they drive in the rain as if it were snow; they drive in the snow as if it were ice and in the sun as if it were raining. They drive slower depending on the level of precipitation, but it starts a level behind every other civilized country.

"I've got the list," my wife said, trying to make things light as we inched along. "I just need you to verify and clarify." Her words came out all singsong-y. Even if they hadn't rhymed, she would have powdered them with cheerfulness.

She knew I was tense. Even after twenty-four years of marriage, I am no good at hiding it. My frustration with life comes at her in bursts of quiet.

"I can't do it while I'm driving," I said, the tension of the quiet now finding its voice.

"It's your birthday," she said.

"It's your party," I said.

"You can't seem to find the time when you are home, or after dinner, or before bed, or during breakfast, or after your Sunday run, or…"

"I'll do it tonight," I said before turning up the sound of a Howard Stern interview on the radio.

The evening had passed as so many others do. I left the office around 5:30 and drove home in traffic and then to another dinner with another couple who are also recently empty-nested, and we had a piece of fish and a glass of wine. I got the house wine because I don't really know much or care much about the wine. And I spent the 125 dollars and I tipped the valet and we drove home in the traffic and the rain.

It was ten o'clock when I got into bed; the baseball game was still bursting from the television when she came upstairs. My eyes were closed in faux sleep.

"I know you're not asleep," she said.

The diagnosis came the next day.

Something had chafed at me as I lay in bed a week earlier, my hand fishing in my pants for the rough patch.

"What are you doing?" my wife asked, never a fan of me with a hand in my pocket, let alone my underwear.

"Something hurts," I told her.

Telling your wife of twenty-plus years that something hurts is akin to asking her if she let the dogs out. It gets a perfunctory response with the impact of a fallen paper clip.

She did not tell me to see a doctor, and I did not tell her I would. And she did not ask again.

But as I searched for this rash or ingrown hair in a place where I would not be comfortable calling a doctor, I did feel what seemed like a third ball, and at first I laughed, but it was too tender.

Now Dr. Ira Katz was telling me it was cancer.

He asked questions in an accusatory manner, of which I was not a fan.

"How long has it been there? When did you first feel it?"

But I heard him asking, "Why didn't you feel it sooner? Why did it take so long to come in?"

And then he told me it had spread, in a way to suggest it was my fault.

He quickly added it was curable, if they attacked it now.

I also didn't like the military references he and the others kept using. We weren't waging war on my nut sack.

The doctor couldn't stop telling me how lucky I was, even though my face was still warm from hearing the word *cancer*, at least as it related to me.

"The good options," he kept saying as he discussed removing my testicles, shooting me with radiation and medication that would make me "feel dreadful" for a while.

"But on the other side of this, you'll feel like your old self," he said. Which didn't seem like such a great option to me.

"But without my balls," I said.

"There is hormone therapy; we've made great progress."

"Do you have both your balls?" I asked.

"I do," he said.

"Do you know what it feels like to not have both balls," I continued until he cut me off.

"Look, if I were a gynecologist, I could still help you get through childbirth even if I wouldn't know what it's like to push out a baby," he said. "Just like I can't relate to the experience of the hundreds of men I've treated over the past twenty years."

I couldn't argue with him and frankly didn't want to. And then I hit him with it. The money question:

"What if I do nothing?" I asked.

"That's not an option," he said.

"I think the choices are still mine," I said back. "My body, my choice?"

"What do you mean?" he asked, cocking his head like a dog hearing a far-off can opener.

"Just what I said. What if I choose no course of action?"

"Then you will die," he said.

"Bad phrasing," I said, "because by the way, we're all gonna die. You may want to add that to your repertoire."

"It will grow," he began slowly, "although I don't know how fast really. I mean, we could test it. But most people come as soon as they feel it, and then it's usually still contained. But yours is not and so it will move faster and you will get sicker, and it will grow and you will get more uncomfortable. And as it metastasizes you will get into real trouble because it will affect multiple organs, multiple treatments, all kinds of problems and complications."

"And pain?" I asked, the real question behind my questions. "How much will this hurt?"

"Pain?"

"Will I be in pain if I do nothing?"

"You came in because you were in pain," he said.

"I was uncomfortable," I said.

"It will start to hurt more," he said. "A lot more."

"Describe it."

"It all depends, but there is the procedure, which isn't pleasant, and then the recovery and then the meds will cause minor problems, nausea, some muscle aches. Hair loss is not unlikely."

I took the literature and scheduled my follow-up appointment.

That night we sat with another couple at another 150-dollar fish and wine dinner.

"Is it undercooked?" my wife asked, pointing her fork at my half-eaten piece of black cod.

"It's fine," I said, but I wasn't hungry. Not because of the diagnosis or the fear of cancer, but my stomach just hurt, as if I'd swallowed a marble and it was trying to pass through my colon. I thought it was mostly in my head; you know, you're told something is broken, and it starts to hurt more.

When I spoke up midway through dinner, my wife looked at me with the surprise of a spouse whose husband just woke from a twenty-year slumber.

The drive home was another replay or another post-dinner analysis, but I found it bothered me less. I always hated these discussions, the analysis of the other couple, what they are doing with their boring lives, the exchange of risotto recipes, their spoiled kids and the great jobs they are getting or the horrible people they are dating. But tonight it was tolerable. Maybe because I knew this discussion would not go on forever, because my forever just got shorter. Even as my stomach gurgled, there was calmness to it as the blabbing became more palatable, knowing it would end soon.

Most mornings in the shower, I would play with the new growth I would find, sort of like that scab you can't stop picking, or that piece of dandruff you might feel in your hair where you need to keep scratching. I would feel it when I put on my underwear and pants, or when I went to the bathroom during the day. But then it would settle into the back of my mind.

The morning was bright with the sun pouring through my windshield. I fumbled for the sunglasses for the first time in what seemed like weeks. A large swath of dust lay across both lenses that I rubbed out on my arm.

Sometimes the warm days would bring me down because they taunted me to go outside and make use of the rare sunshine in February. But now it was welcoming, and I looked forward to a weekend hike and some work for a potential client.

The doctor's office left a message telling me I'd missed my appointment and asking me to call back to reschedule.

I erased it immediately and pretended like it never came.

"What's wrong with you this time," my wife said as I came in from the backyard with the dogs.

"What do you mean, this time?"

"You're limping," she said.

But she got distracted when the phone rang.

Weeks passed and I began to wonder, what is the doctor's obligation? He knows I have cancer, he knows I will die sooner rather than later if not treated, yet his office stopped calling after only three tries? Is that all I'm worth? I know they can't force me to come in, but still, shouldn't they be trying a little harder?

I soon became an expert on my body and its functions and fluids. Every ache that seemed odd or new, every bowel movement that hurt, the way food tasted, the sounds my stomach made as I lay in bed with Terry sleeping next to me.

I enjoyed having this secret all to myself. At dinner when friends asked how I stayed in shape, it was the first time I realized my pants weren't fitting. I had stopped working out and felt less healthy, but something inside of me was eating away at the fat or the muscle, I didn't know which, but I was losing weight. Not in huge drops, I only weighed 175 at my peak, but little by little the pants grew on me, the collar on my shirt hung open, not quite another belt loop, but it was moving in that direction.

"How does it feel?"

I was surprised by the question as I ran my fingers over my stomach, thinking I felt another protrusion, like the one I saw in the bathroom earlier that day.

I must have looked surprised because Rick, our company attorney, asked the question again.

"This was the longest negotiation I ever remember you sitting through," he said. "You showed more patience than I have ever seen."

I didn't ever recall feeling this good about a deal, or more successful. We had worked long hours to get this signed. And while the fruits of this work, the real money, wouldn't start coming until the out years, I felt a sense of accomplishment. Years three and four of this deal were years I would not see, although I really didn't know how long it would take for this cancer to kill me, but I assumed it would be sooner than that.

The following month a reminder for my next dentist appointment arrived on my desk. I looked at the date, two weeks in the future. I would of course be around for it, but did I want to go? I didn't expect to be around for my next one, six months later, so why go to this one? I remember the sign in the office from when I was a kid: "You don't have to brush all of your teeth, only the ones you want to keep." The goal is to keep your teeth your whole life. Well, put a checkmark by it; there's no need to go beyond that.

The invitations for my fiftieth birthday went out. I'd never reviewed the invite list. Terry just got sick of waiting and decided the date would come and go whether I spent the time reviewing the people I liked or didn't like, the names of those we no longer spent time with and the people who were more obligation than preference.

Planning a party outdoors seems to be something you do if you are naturally lucky or stupid. But Terry always planned things outside, and it was always the sunniest day of the year.

"But this is my birthday," I protested, "not yours. Maybe God will realize it's for me and make it rain."

Terry answered with some long, slightly humorous answer that I mostly missed because for the first time I'd invoked God, a person who rarely had a seat at our table, and I wondered.

Feeling closer to death or the end or the whatever, my focus on what it might be like would hit me at odd times, when people said things invoking religion or heaven and hell or even the word *die*, like "I almost died" after seeing a scary movie or being embarrassed in a public setting. The words would set me off on a course of thought that sometimes turned gory, like thinking about bugs in my casket and what if I wasn't really dead and I had to get out and I couldn't, like that girl I once read about. And then I would go over every indiscretion from the past fifty years and wonder if it really mattered, if someone else saw what I did and would then put me in judgment for it.

I found myself sitting in our children's bedrooms, stuck in time, old posters on the wall of basketball players no longer in the league, ticket stubs from long-forgotten concerts, a presidential library to their achievements before they left our house.

A "Grrrrr" sound coming from the corner of my son's room startled me. I reached over behind his desk to find a small plastic spaceman that hadn't been touched in probably ten years. Maybe longer? What do we do with all this discarded stuff? What do we do with pictures, the toys or clothes of people after they lose their usefulness?

The toy roared again in my hands. I flipped it over to see an on/off switch protruding from the spaceman's butt. I moved it on, then off, and the arms moved slowly, just a touch, as if a long-dead item had one final thing to say.

Maybe this is how we die.

I'd never thought too much about it, the whole body and soul, another life, another place, thing. Except maybe on those rare occasions when I found myself inside a place of worship, a holiday, a wedding when I was too bored to listen and the sounds of the place just made me wonder. For the most part I was too busy being annoyed with this life to worry about another one. But now these topics invaded my head like uninvited relatives and they didn't leave. They just sat there between my ears as I played with this dead, or dying, toy in my hands. I felt tired at that moment and thought maybe, like this toy, we just run out of gas. Maybe our batteries die and we end up on the floor or in a corner, our structure still there, but everything inside is all turned off. Our on/off switch still in the on position but nothing moves; inside it's all hollow and quiet.

Or maybe, after months or even years, we move again, even slightly, just a smidge. The gears and switches of our mind and body connect up in a moment and like some small big bang, and we move or sit up or think or whine or bark or yell. Maybe we aren't awake, something akin to sleepwalking.

Death, which always looked to me like a trapdoor, a way to escape the troubles of today without having to explain, now brought some sense of not dread, but fear. What if it's scary, that moment, the days after? The physical pain of the coming months wasn't the problem; it was afterward when I would really be alone, even more than I was now.

The following week it was nineteen-year-old son who was playing with the dead toy.

"What do you think he would have done?" Nathan asked his sister.

"Where did you find this?" she asked.

"It was on my desk."

The children had come home for my funeral. The call from their mother was agitated, though not screaming. Most likely she'd taken a sedative, they assumed.

"The police are here," Terry said to our son, the same words she used to open the discussion with our daughter.

She waited after saying the first sentence long enough for them to ask why.

"It was a bus," she continued.

The suspense was too much for them, each asking her, "What are you telling me?"

She finally got it out, telling them about the crash, how the bus ran a red light, pushing my car into oncoming traffic. They didn't know if I died from the initial impact or whether it was the second car or the third. It didn't matter. Their father was dead and this was that phone call that they didn't expect to hear for another twenty years.

"He didn't live very long after the crash," the police officer guaranteed her. "He was gone by the time we arrived."

And now a week later, the shock still reverberating around the house, the siblings, who admitted they hadn't spoken to me in the weeks leading up to the accident, were talking about the blue felt diary filled with my familiar left-handed script.

"Do you think Mom knew?" she asked her brother.

"And didn't tell us?" he said. "It's possible. I don't know what kind of secret pact a husband and wife make after their kids go off to college, but this isn't something you hide."

"Why did they stay in this big house?" she asked.

"Had to be depressing," he said.

"Nothing has changed," she said. "Those are the same sheets on my bed from high school."

"Do you think they ever used these rooms?" he asked.

"Dad must have if his diary was sitting on your desk," she said.

"He could have moved in here, for all we know," he said. "Maybe after the kids go away you worry less about how it looks and more about what you want. It's great, you can sleep in a different bed, stay in a different part of the house if you want privacy. Have your own bathroom?"

"I never thought about it before," she said.

"About what?"

"About them," she said. "You know, their lives."

"She didn't know he was dying," my son said.

"Do you believe her?"

"Why would she lie?"

"Maybe she knew and didn't want us to worry," my daughter said. "Or maybe she is embarrassed he never told her."

"This can't be real," he said, raising the blue book, the covers splayed open. "Maybe he was writing a story."

"A story," she said. "This was the world's most uncreative man and suddenly he's writing short stories about middle-aged men who lie about having cancer."

"That wasn't what the story was about," Nathan said. "It's about a man who didn't want to live."

"It's about a man who kept secrets," she said.

"It's about a man who wanted something that was his own," he said, before tossing the book onto the vacant bed. "Do we tell her?"

"She must have known," she said again.

"It was his secret to tell or to keep," he said.

"Then why did he write it down?" she said. "He wanted us to find out."

"But why?" he said.

"It's sort of a dicky move," she said. "Telling us, after he died, that he didn't love us enough to want to live."

"We weren't a part of this equation," he said.

"Then why did he write it all down?" she said.

"We weren't meant to know."

The doorbell, a familiar childhood sound, rang out, which set off a chain reaction of barking dogs and ringing phones.

They both left the room and prepared for another round of discussions with people from their childhood who would recount an anecdote about their dad and then say something completely innocuous like what a good guy he was.

But instead of a neighbor, it was a white box with red postal stripes and an envelope.

It had been delivered, but the delivery person didn't wait for a signature or anything. The envelope had their father's name on it. Inside the blank business envelope was a typed letter with one line:

Office belongings: Peter Wolving.

They took off the top of the unsecured box to find a stack of books and folders, loose papers, and a bound appointment calendar, the same type I had kept for years, unwilling to move to something electronic.

Their mother put her hand to her lips and went back into the kitchen. The brother and sister began fingering through the last of their father's belongings. The son flipped pages in my calendar, a voyeuristic thrill and fear.

He opened it to the final week of my life.

"Who is Doctor Katz?" he said.

"Never heard of him," his sister said. "Why?"

"Mom, who is Doctor Katz?" he yelled. "Dad had an appointment today."

HIROMI YOSHIDA
TV DINNER

Snowbound nights when my PhD-seeking mom
decided to give herself a break; and me,
and Mei-Mei a treat, I relished
each steaming Swanson TV dinner item, nestled
in crinkled aluminum foil, an American *obento* box:

Veal parmigiana meatloaf
    smothered in tomato sauce and cheese;
Mashed potatoes,
    fluffy white and buttery yellow;
Green peas,
    ultimate food for kids
to play with;

    Apple strudel,
    central dessert delight,
      ensconced in tiniest
aluminum square,
beckoning
    baked jewel, apple of
      my hungry eye.

Nothing compared to Mom's
oven-baked Scotch eggs, of
course, but those TV

dinners enabled me and my baby
sister to see
who could stick

a
pea
on
every
fork
prong
okay.

JEAN VARDA
DROPS OF MERCY
Living with the California drought

one drop for your hand
warmly holding mine
one for each of your eyes
how blue they are and kind
one drop for your life how
long and interesting and so
easily forgotten, one drop
for each coffee pot that holds
the steamy black liquid
that so relaxes you,
ten drops for my pony
as she stands in the mud
patiently waiting for the rain
three drops for the birds
in the parking lot, eating
the dry crumbs I toss
drinking from a shallow
puddle left from the ice
spilled from an Arby's cup
twelve drops for the humming
birds, their long beaks
drinking the last of the sugar
water as their wings beat
one thousand times a minute
and the last drop is your breath
how it struggles in and out
of your lungs, grabbing
on to life, because that
is all it knows

PETER BREYER
FIFTY-TWO YEARS LATER

Leaning on the front gate of my rental house in Newark, I am alarmed to sense a man standing close behind me. Turning, I peer into a dark face with penetrating eyes. "Give me your money!" he says. With his right hand on a gun stuck in his waist, he repeats the command.

"You got to be kidding," I say.

"Give me all your money," he demands again, this time more forcefully. Realizing the guy is serious, slowly I reach for my wallet with my back still facing the thief. My wife, who is cleaning the outdoor stairway several feet away, senses something wrong and approaches the two of us. When she sees me reach for my wallet, she screams, "Get out of here! You're not getting anything from us!" With a hand broom she begins hitting the man.

"Mil, he's got a gun," I yell.

"I don't care, get out of here," she continues as she intensifies her blows.

Seeming impervious to her strikes, the man increases his demands. "Give me all your money!"

In the commotion, I lose my balance and fall to one knee and fear the man will shoot my wife. I know I have to give the guy something. Seeing my wallet, he yells, "Give it to me."

"No, you're not getting my wallet," I shout back. Quickly, I yank some bills with my right hand and hold it up. He grabs the money and, in a flash, he runs down the street.

Little do I realize that the real action is yet to unfold. It starts with Mildred asking me, "How much did he get?" No, she really didn't ask but yelled. Sheepishly, I tell her, "Not sure, but around a hundred and forty."

Caesar, the man doing tile repair for me in the house, appears as well as people from across the street. That's when Mildred really gets started on her tirade. "I'm sick of these black men acting like this. Why the hell doesn't he get a job?" she yells for the entire crowd to hear.

"Calm down, Mama," Caesar said. "Not worth getting shot for a few dollars."

"I don't care about the money!" she retorted sharply. My beautiful wife is still pumped full of adrenaline, her fists clenching and unclenching. I can see the hard line of her jaw, how she is gritting her teeth against the smooth softness of her cheek. "We have worked so hard and come so far. We don't need to be doing this. Let him work like we all do," again she yells, this time for the benefit of the people down the street.

I don't want to remind Mildred that most of the street people who appear don't work. They mostly freeload and do drugs.

"Babe, it's okay. I couldn't take a chance. He could have shot you," I say in an effort to calm her down.

With a fury in her eyes and her mouth drawn tight, she shouts, "I don't care, you hear me? I'm sick of these men acting like this. They're a discredit to all of us."

"The guy could have shot you, Mama," Caesar repeats.

Mildred continues on her rampage against the thief. There's no shutting her down once she gets started, like a runaway train.

All I can think of is the 140 dollars I just lost and my cowardly behavior in handing it over. I reach for my phone to call the police. We wait and talk about the things I should have done during this thirty-second assault.

After hearing the news, my immigrant tenants from Ghana come out of the house.

"Did they get the rent money I just gave you?" one asked.

"No, that was in my back pocket." Ah, so I didn't give him all my money after all. Mildred is not appeased at the news. She is still so affronted that we were robbed.

Her new name, Mama, is striking to me. It's a Spanish expression for older women. My wife is seventy-five, as am I, but a young seventy-five, for sure. But I never thought of her as Mama.

We sit on the outdoor steps of our house for another hour and a half. It's 6:00 p.m. On this Sunday evening the block is quiet. The street people have retreated for the moment, recharging themselves for their regular nightly appearance, which usually starts at around 9:00 and lasts until midnight or later. That's according to my tenants, since by then I am safely in my nice retirement condo in central New Jersey. But I also confirm their presence by the dozens of half-drunk soda and water bottles that litter the front of my house on the mornings that I come by. I have yet to understand why someone would buy something to drink and leave half of it untouched. So, I dutifully empty the bottles and throw them in the trash barrel.

The police don't come. "They never come when you call them," Prince, one of my tenants, says. "This is Newark."

When I told the despatcher on the 911 line that I was unhurt and the thief ran away, my report must have fallen low on their priority list.

At 11:30, half asleep, I hear my cell phone ring. "This is the Newark Police. I understand that you reported an incident this afternoon."

"Yes," I say as I proceed to explain what happened. I soon realize that the woman on the phone has no interest in what happened but wants to know the address again so she can refer me to the proper police precinct. She hangs up and promises to call back. At 12:00, I receive another call and am told to report the incident at the police precinct on Lincoln Street. I thank her and go back to sleep.

Instead, as I am trying to fall asleep, I think of all the precautions I should take. Yes, I will carry a big knife. I could have turned around and stabbed the guy in the back. Yeah, in his back by his heart.

But do I really want to kill somebody over 140 bucks?

By morning, I decide on Mace, which I buy at the nearest Walmart. One can on me and one in the car. If I had had it, I could have turned around and sprayed the guy. It's nasty stuff and incapacitates you for twenty minutes according to the instructions.

I sit in the police station on Lincoln Street. It is shift change, so I'm told to wait outside. Half an hour later, I can enter, and after telling the desk officer what happened, he instructs me to sit outside and wait. "An officer will come and escort you downtown." Forty minutes later an officer, Vargos, appears. Short and stocky as is virtually every police officer I see in the precinct. I think they discriminate against tall, thin men and women.

I explain what happened. He takes notes. "Okay, come with me."

"Where?"

"Downtown to Robbery," he says.

He explains they have one building for domestic violence, one for robbery, and another for homicide. "No, don't bring your car since you won't be able to park."

I sit in the back of his SUV police car. The seat is hard vinyl. There are no door handles. Once I'm seated, I'm locked in. "Want some air?" he asks.

When I say, "yes," he rolls the back windows down only to be covered with thick plastic barriers with thin air strips cut in. I'm also locked from the front seat by a thick plastic barrier. *Crap, I'm locked in here.* Being claustrophobic, I begin to panic. *Relax*, I tell myself, *it will be okay.*

We stop at my house, which he refers to as the crime scene. He checks for surveillance cameras. "You got to be kidding," I tell him.

"They'd be gone in a day."

I get back in my prison. As we pull away two of my street people acquaintances see me through the plastic window guards with slits and wave. They undoubtedly think I'm being arrested. I wave and give them a thumbs-up. They smile and wave back. Maybe I have gained a little status on the street for being in the back of the police car.

"Yes, he had a gun. Yes, my wife hit him. No, I never saw him before. Yes, he ran toward Park Avenue," and on and on...

"Next time this happens, what if I hit him with my hammer?" I ask.

"No, don't do that, just call your wife," one of them says and they all laugh.

They make an official recording of my story, I sign a statement, and Vargos drives me back to the Lincoln precinct where my van is parked. Thankfully I didn't get a ticket, and I return to my house to work on my basement renovation. More vigilant now, I look at everyone I encounter on the street.

A week later, I am mentally prepared for the next attack. My Mace is handy and I will not retreat in fear. But mostly, I keep thinking about my wife and the pain she experienced in seeing this black man engage in this behavior. The oldest of five children of parents who were part of the great migration from Mississippi, she grew up in a small town on the outskirts of Chicago. Her father worked in the mills, had a truck to do hauling on weekends, and was a stout member of his AME church. Her mother, who married at eighteen, worked one and sometimes two jobs. They never had much, and sometimes the coal was gone late in the winter.

But never would they accept a handout. Welfare for them was an indignity that reduced a family to disgrace. Mildred is a hard-ass proud black woman who never expected anything from anybody, and expects the same standard from others. Once, after giving an apple to a black panhandler on the New York subway, she was indignant when he threw it back at her.

Being married to a white man has had its share of difficulty for her. Not from her family, but friends. More so in the past when a black woman with a white man was seen as a sellout. "She's not really black," some would say and others would think.

But what do others know about what a person feels? When we pass a group of inmates in orange suits cleaning trash by the side of the highway, I sense her pain when they are all black. Once in her job as an inspector for a children's unit for juvenile offenders, Mildred came back in tears. She said she thought she was on a slave ship. Whenever we go into a public setting, she is mentally counting how many black people are present. We watch the evening crime report, and she turns it off when they show a black perpetrator. She feels a burden of being responsible for what black people do. "Why do we have to do all these things?" she asks me.

On a recent trip to the West Coast, she was happy when she saw white homeless people in Santa Monica. "It's not only us," she said.

I find her bravery in the face of danger more admirable considering the violence in her own family. Her mother and two relatives were shot and killed at a wedding before her eyes. The shooter was declared insane and did some time in a mental hospital before being released. The memory of her holding her unconscious mother as she lay dying has never left her. Yet, she was willing to challenge this armed robber without knowing the outcome. "I wouldn't have minded so much being robbed by a white man," she said. "But a black man!"

A guest preacher at our church the following Sunday referred to Luke 18 when Jesus blessed the children. He talked about his own granddaughter and what she will face as a black woman, given a high percentage of assaults in the African-American community. "We (meaning he and his wife) will support her to become a strong black woman, proud of who she is."

This led me to think about my wife, a beautiful, proud black woman who has never forgotten who she is. She is open to all and can count white women as some of her closest friends, but she is always aware that she's a black person in a dominant white culture.

In times of stress our true natures emerge. When people now ask me what I'm doing in Newark and why I keep this house, I have to tell them that sometimes discomfort leads to greater rewards. The type that can only come about by leaving our zones of safety and participating in a way of life experienced by millions of people in inner-city America.

So, maybe being robbed in Newark wasn't so bad after all, paying $140.00 for such an important lesson. It has heightened an awareness in me, even after fifty-two years, of who my wife really is, not only as my partner in life, but as a human being.

She is even more exquisite now than on the day she was my bride.

ALEXANDER PAYNE MORGAN
BISTRO SAVANNAH

I order the grits and shrimp and get
a prank on my plate.
It has to be.

A tiny mound of yellow grits
with four miniscule shrimp arranged in a wheel
and three bold diagonals of asparagus,
I suppose to impress me with their "color" and "drama."

I'm not immune to the charms of culinary flair, but
what kind of *Savannah* meal is this?

Start with magnitude:
forty makes more sense than four.
Don't peel them and—
it being only civil to let a creature see its fate—
leave the heads on too.

The shrimp should be served in a bucket,
ready to fight back when nabbed,
and we need a hole in the middle of the table to receive
the inedible portions of the corpses.

Those grits should start out white
in a bowl of sufficient capacity,
at least a quart.
Butter on the side, cheese appreciated.

Who ordered this chardonnay wine?
How about some old-fashioned sweet tea,
reinforced discreetly with bourbon,
kissed with mint, cradled in crushed ice
like Mother's basic summer-evening libation?

No guest should rise from a Southern table
fit for anything but staggering off to slumber.

(cont)

Leaving hungry,
offended,
I have to uncover the roots of this gastronomic mendacity.
I arrange a discreet moment with one of the waitstaff.
I knew it!
The owner's from Ohio.

Morgan

BUS STATION PRAYER
Carrolton, Georgia, 1967

Dear God, let us get on with no trouble.
In the bus station, the family huddles,
eyes cast down, father, mother, daughter, son.
They don't know their place, the signs taken down.

In the bus station, the family huddles,
Black family. I almost forgot that part.
They don't know their place, the signs taken down.
Station not segregated anymore.

The Black family, *they* don't forget that part.
As they huddle, they pray they're in their place.
Station not segregated anymore,
but who knows what White traps are in the room now?

They huddle. They whisper. They feel misplaced.
I'm a White kid confused. What do I see?
Something white and dark left trapped in the room now,
what I never saw when the signs were up.

I'm a White kid displaced by what I see—
downcast eyes, father, mother, daughter, son—
what I should have seen when the signs were up.
Dear God, let us get on with no trouble.

Morgan

PERSISTENCE

I visit her grave in Bonaventure Cemetery
once a year in April,
my mother's mother,
the slave owner's daughter,
Beatrice on this stone.
We called her Granny.

I held her hand many times,
a hand that held the hand
that blessed the lacerations
to make the fear
to force the labor.

I still smell terror in the Savannah air.

It's as real as the hydrogen sulfide
from the pulpwood processing plant,
used to be just across the river, the plant
whose "rotten egg" stinks
we joked about as children
and breathed.

Granny talked about her daddy in whispers.
We children waited like hungry dogs
for scraps and bites dropped
by mistake in our hearing.
We snatched up the dripping morsels, ran
to gulp them down
before they could be taken back
or forgotten:
He had seven White daughters, my grandmother
the baby of the seven.
After "the war," they'd had to sweep their own
veranda; for shame, he made them do it after
dark.
Her sisters locked her in a closet; she never could
stand darkness
after that.

(cont)

He'd sold his other children.

Like a Dark-Ages monk
copying Lucretius,
I took down Granny's words
without understanding them.

I look now
sixty years later
at Granny's grave.

I walk around Savannah.

Downtown's gentrified:
    bistros
    gift shops
    ghost tours
    the Savannah School of Art and Design
        with students from
            Cincinnati
            Minneapolis
            Newark
            Detroit.

When I was a kid,
Damned Yankees weren't welcome;
now they flow in a flood, but
what were we afraid of?

They don't change us.
We are as we were.

A Black family waits in the bus station,
grouped tense on the colored side. Signs
down, but they
know.

Three old White guys at the Waffle House
won't give their order to the Black waitress,
hold out for a White one.

(cont)

At the library, a young White writer
wows us with his eloquent stories,
then repeats the old ones
about "outside agitators"
and "lying liberal journalists,"
assures us "the colored people
have always been treated
just fine."

Morgan

ODE TO BLUEBERRIES
After "Ode To Tomatoes" by Pablo Neruda

Late summer
already contemplates giving way to fall.
I would be blue like depression,
but this moment
is sweet and crisp,
blue like a berry.

In August,
suddenly,
the blueberry
apparates at groceries in grand five-pound boxes,
offers mounds of glee in farmers' markets,
draws me to sweet-talk Janice
into four-hour drives
north
just to kidnap pounds and pounds
promised to the freezer,
but resting rinsed
on the kitchen counter among
dullard vegetables,
oafish meats,
treacherous starches,
it revels in the force of its own coaxing,
compels its own consumption,
doesn't deign
to plastic freezer boxes.

This blue celebrity (cont)

savors its short life
like a butterfly. It offers itself,
deranged like a saint
soliciting ugly execution:
mastication, digestion…
It seeks to suffer
its special ecstasy.

Lofty blue reward
in cool
stellar clusters,
we introduce it
to the excitable vanilla ice cream,
the philosophical chocolate,
or simmer it in pots with sugars,
pour it into pies,
mashing its perfect spherical geometry,
then pile it with plebian Cool Whip,
that white fluffy nothing,
or haughty whipped cream,
that fat roué,
smothering
our tolerant blue-blooded guest
in exuberant excessive sweetness.

The blueberry is no mere vegetable,
no common apple,
no eager grape or
silly banana.
The blueberry holds itself regal,
can't be shamed
by our vulgar compulsion
to sugarcoat perfection.

Blueberry,
celebrity of this sad-sweet moment
at the end of summer,
this two weeks of sweet-tart completion,
shows us the splendor
of blue aristocracy
and sweet martyrdom.

Morgan

Elizabeth Standing Bear
Holly Patterson
Valedictorian
Class of 2020

I was sitting on the porch swing on my glassed in front porch around 9 pm watching the storm, enjoying the rain on the tin roof, when I saw a vehicle pause out on the road, the interior light came on as the door opened—too far for me to identify anyone—as they put something out and drove off.

Great! Another unwanted cat or dog abandoned on a stormy spring night. A flash of lightening allowed me to glimpse the creature scurry into the brush on the far side of the road, headed toward the broken down barn. Tomorrow I would have to deal with it.

With a sigh, I went into the house and took myself to bed; the sound of rain, the storm, and the smell of rain-bruised lilacs inviting sleep.

The next morning I waited until 10 am to allow the sun to dry the field, and carried a small jar of milk and an open can of tuna in a baggy down the lane to the road and on the narrow path west toward the grey broken down barn.

I love that old barn. It has character even as its roof leans toward the South, its door leans against it in the weeds, and some of its walls are see-through, so many boards missing. Some family say I should tear it down, it's an eyesore, it's a danger, but I haven't the heart. My great grandfather built it and my family farmed here until there was no one left to farm, the young people going off to college, to their own lives, to marriage and children, scattered as cottonwood fluff to all the corners of the country. Just looking at the barn, hollyhocks coming up along the east wall, made me smile. I couldn't even consider tearing it down.

When I stepped through the door opening there was a scurry to my right. The roof was good enough that it was dry inside, in spite of last night's storm. The scurry sound repeated so I sat down on the bench near the door and stayed still, whistling softly, waiting.

"Kitty, kitty," I tried. Nothing.

I whistled some more.

"Puppy, puppy, come, puppy." Nothing. Then to my total shock a face peeped out from a stall. It was a little girl, about five or so in age, dressed in a cotton dress and sneakers.

"Hi, honey," I said. "What's your name? Are you hungry?" She ducked back into the stall, then emerged carrying a small backpack and a stuffed dog. Tentatively she came toward me, her eyes big, brown, scared.

I patted the bench beside me and she sat down. I opened the jar of milk and handed it to her. She drank it straight down.

"What's your name, honey?" I repeated.

"Holly," she said softly, so softly I had to strain to hear her. The dish and the tuna wouldn't work in this situation.

"Come, Holly. Let's go to the house and I'll make you some breakfast." I helped her put her backpack on and held her hand as we took the path to the road and the lane to the house.

In my kitchen after using the bathroom and washing her hands, Holly put her backpack on the floor, her dog on one chair, and climbed up on a chair at the table. She was so small she could barely see over the table edge. I got her a cushion, raising her up to a better level.

More milk, toast, an egg over easy, and a bowl of peaches later Holly was at last filled up.

"What were you doing in my barn?" I asked gently.

"It was raining. The barn was dry. There was hay to sleep on," she answered, matter of factually.

"Did you sleep okay? Were you warm enough?"

"After the storm stopped. It was very loud. Then there were mice watching me."

"Did they scare you?"

"No. I like mice. We have a tank full of them at kindygarten."

"How did you get out here? We are miles from town."

"Mom and Jim drove me." My blood boiled. Here was this sweet child put out on a stormy night like an unwanted puppy, by her mother! And who was this Jim? Some people! What was my next move? I took a deep breath to calm myself.

Holly looked sleepy so I led her to the living room where she curled up on the sofa with her dog and was soon asleep. I fetched her backpack and opened it on the coffee table.

There was a pair of shorts and a top, another dress, several pairs of socks and undies, all clean and neatly folded. Someone loved this child. Was her mom in trouble? In danger from Jim? There was a storybook: "Are You My Mom?" well worn, in which Holly had written her name: Holly Martin, Age 5, in purple crayon.

The child stirred, then slept on. Quietly I replaced her things in the pack and headed for the kitchen phone.

Speed dial got me where I needed to be.

"Cathy, this is Helen. Is Sheriff in?"

"Yes, Helen, let me get him for you." I waited. Cathy came back on the line: "Helen, he is tied up at the present. Can I have him call you back?"

"Yes. It is somewhat urgent, but not an emergency," I said.

"Wait, here he is now."

"Sheriff Patterson," he said. I loved the deep rich sound, the reassuring sound, of his voice.

"John, it's Helen."

"Are you canceling our dinner plans?" he chuckled. I had cancelled the last time we had a "date."

"No, John, but you may want to come out here as soon as you can."

"Are you okay?"

"Yes." I was reluctant to go into details over the phone. Small town and all that. I would give him the story face to face. "How soon can you be here?"

"I'll come right away."

"Thank you, John." I waited and stewed, the child slept on, until his car appeared in my driveway, where I met him on the side porch. We kissed in greeting and sat on the wicker couch, while I filled him in about Holly.

"I have a feeling the mom may be in danger, but not much to tell you that will help you find her," I said, sadly.

John made some notes in his notebook. Time. Direction the vehicle was traveling. Holly's name, and age. "I need to talk to Holly," he said standing. Together we went into the house. We watched her sleeping for a minute, then I woke her gently.

"Holly, wake up honey." She startled when she saw the uniformed, armed man. John sat down on the floor beside the couch.

"Hi, Holly, I'm Sheriff Patterson." He offered his hand and she put her hand, her tiny trusting hand, in his big mitt. "Can you tell me about yesterday?" He asked. "Can you tell me how you came to be taking shelter in Helen's barn?"

"It was raining. Hard. Lightening showed me the barn, so I went there and went in out of the rain."

"What were you doing on the road?"

"Jim stopped the car. He told mom to get me out. So she opened the door and helped me out."

"Why do you think she did that?"

"Cause Jim told her."
"Jim told her to put you out of the car?"
"Yes."
"Do you think she wanted to do that?"
"No. She was crying. Jim slapped her."
"Do you know Jim's last name?"
"No."
"Can you tell me what he looks like?"

Holly leaned out and unzipped her pack. She opened the storybook and turned the pages. A photo fell out. She handed it to John. It was one of those photo booth strips showing Holly with a man and a woman.

"Is this your mom?"
"Yes. And that's Jim."
"Where were you going in the car?"
"Jim said we were going to Disneyland." Her face got sad and tears started. "He lied, didn't he?"
"Where did you start this trip?"
"Home. I know my address and phone number. We had to learn it for kindygarten."
"Very good, Holly," I said. "Tell me what you know." She recited in a singsong voice what she had learned for school. "You are such a smart little girl." I sat down beside her and put my arms around her. John had made note of it and was in the kitchen on the phone with dispatch. Phone in his hand, he came and sat beside us.

"Holly, what kind of car does Jim drive?"
"A black one," she answered.
"How many doors are there?" She held up her hand, counting finger by finger.
"Four," she answered.
"Was there anything special about the car you remember?"
"There was a window in the roof. At night I could see the stars. Last night I could see lightening."
"Was there anything you remember about the inside of the car?"
"Well…my car seat. It has Hello Kitty on it." She smiled. "I like Hello Kitty."
"What about the front of the car, where mom and Jim sit."
"Just gray seats."
"Do you know what license plates are?"
"Yes. They are metal with letters and numbers on them, on the

front and back of the car."

"What color are they?

"Red and white with black letters and numbers. They are funny because the letters spell cat, only backwards: T-A-C. I don't remember the numbers."

"Very good, Holly." John repeated the car's description and T-A-C into the phone before he put it down. "Holly, was your mom afraid of Jim?" he asked.

"I don't know. He made her cry. He hit her."

"We are going to do our best to find her," John said. "Helen, walk me to my car?"

"I'll be right back, Holly," I said, and went out with John.

"We need to call in CPS," John said, leaning against the car.

"No, John, no," I slipped into his arms.

"You know we must involve them."

"Not yet. Please. Holly will be fine with me, you know that."

"I know you'll take good care of her, Helen. It's a legality. I want to protect you." I backed away and dug in my heels, ready for an all-out fight.

"I'll be fine! Leave her here for now. See if the investigation turns up the car, Jim, or mom."

John sighed, sensing my determination, avoiding a battle. "Okay, 48 hours. I'll be in constant touch."

"Thank you," I hugged him hard.

"Love you, Helen."

"Love you, too, John." He got into his car and drove off.

While Jim and mom had a 15 hour head start, they didn't know how helpful Holly was to the early investigation. By the time John reached his office, Holly's address three counties away had been checked out and cleared. They had learned Jim's last name from a piece of mail found in the trash and finger prints found in the bathroom were awaiting for an identification/verification, if it was his real name, if a match was on file somewhere. Computers were sorting car registrations looking for a vehicle description with the beginning letters T-A-C. In under two hours John had enough information to issue an all-points bulletin for a person of interest in the state and surrounding states. They must proceed with caution, assuming Holly's mom, Sara Martin, was in danger.

At last the car was spotted getting gas. But Jim was alone. The Hello Kitty car seat was found in a dumpster behind the Save-More in our town. The car with only Jim in it was 800 miles east, no sign of Sara

Martin, when it was stopped because a taillight was out.

The officer gave Jim a warning ticket and pretended not to hear the noise coming from the trunk. Jim drove off not suspecting anyone was on his tail.

Fearing Jim might harm his captive, a road block was planned and the car was surrounded 50 miles later. Jim threw his hands out the window pretending to surrender, then rammed his way out of the stop. The chase was on.

Knowing Sara Martin was most likely in the trunk, officers held back, keeping the chase slow but keeping the car in sight on the ground and from the air with a highway patrol plane. When the pilot reported gunshot flashes another road block with nail strips was quickly arranged. With four flats the car slid into a guard rail and Jim ran into nearby woods, disappearing in the dark.

The trunk was opened. Jim had fired a gun through the back seat six times. Holly's mom was bound and gagged with duct tape. She was shot dead.

Officers had called for K-9 and followed Jim into the woods. John got the call at 4 am. Holly's mom Sara Martin was dead. Jim was in custody two states away.

John called me about 10 am and asked if he could come to lunch. Of course I said yes, eager to hear from him exactly what was going on. I met him on the side porch. He had a box he set down and hugged me tight.

"Sara Martin is dead," he said into my hair.

"Oh, John, I'm sorry about that," tears in my eyes.

"Where's Holly?" he asked.

"In the new barn."

"Good. We need to talk out of ear shot." He opened the box and took out a booster seat. "Let's put this in your truck." Together we walked to my old green truck and opened the passenger door. John held me as he leaned in and placed the booster seat in the middle of the bench seat.

"Tell me what you are thinking, John." I turned and climbed upon the truck seat, with his help. My eyes were red. He handed me his handkerchief and held me close.

"My staff poured over Sara's address book, making calls, looking for next of kin. It seems there is no one. Do you still want to keep CPS out of this?"

"Now more than ever."

"Good. I made an appointment for 2 pm with Judge Wallace. I

told her the circumstances. She will grant you 60 days temporary custody. After lunch we will go to town to see her."

"Thus the necessary booster seat."

John shrugged. "You may need to go to town for groceries, clothes for Holly, many reasons." He grew thoughtful.

"Yes, John?" I broke into his silence.

"The coroner will release Sara Martin to Weavers Funeral Home later this week. I think we should wait to tell Holly her mom is dead until we can show her, until she can say goodbye."

"I agree. Let's get Holly from the barn and have lunch." I hopped down.

"What is she doing in the barn?" John asked.

"The cat decided to have her kittens in a nesting box, a favorite of one old red biddy. We were worried the hen might harm the kittens, so Holly is standing guard. She is fascinated with the kittens."

We found Holly sitting a stool in front of the nesting box, one hand gently petting the newborns, the other pushing the squawking hen away. John scooped up the hen and locked her in the tack room where she could cause no harm.

"Come, Holly. The kittens will be safe now. Let's have lunch, then we have to go to town," he said.

Holly slipped her hand into John's as we walked to the house.

"How can we go to town without my Hello Kitty car seat?" she asked.

"I got you a booster seat," John answered.

We took Holly to Pam's Day Care. She was excited to meet other children to have a play date, and we headed for the courthouse.

Judge Wallace, whom I had known for years, was glad to approve my temporary custody application.

Later that week John and I took Holly to Weavers Funeral Home so she could see her mom and say goodbye. It helped, her seeing her mom, for Holly to understand Sara was gone and not coming back. She knew Jim was in jail a long ways off and couldn't hurt Sara or her again. She cried. She kissed her mom's cheek. I held her on my lap during the brief ceremony. She said goodbye one last time, then fell asleep in my arms. She was at last able to relax, the tension drained from her tiny body.

The rest of our 60 days was busy.

John proposed, again, as he had several times over the past year. I loved him so much. I had only resisted because of our ages, me 62 and him 65. Who needed a piece of paper at our ages? We were married within the month. Holly was our flower girl.

Thinking it might take some time, Sheriff and Mrs. John Patterson immediately applied to adopt one five year old girl. Holly Martin became Holly Martin Patterson before the first day of first grade in September.

After we were married, John moved to the farm. A scanner and radio were installed on the counter in the pantry. A door was installed from the pantry to the back parlor. It became his office, with a table and chair for Holly so she could do her homework, color, play, activities he shared as time allowed.

We were stronger every day, as a family. When Holy was 16 she came to us. A school science project stirred her interest. She wanted to locate her biological father. John took a DNA swab from Holly and began the process of trying to locate him.

It didn't take long to discover Jim, who was incarcerated two states away, was Holly's birth father. John and I sat Holly down and told her. She wanted to see him.

John and Holly planned a road trip. Together they visited the prison. Separated by glass, talking over speakers, John set up the recorder, Holly asked the tough questions.

"Why did you make mom put me out of the car?"

"I never wanted kids. I wanted her. I loved her. But not you." he answered.

"How long were you together when she told you she was pregnant with me?"

"Three years. She knew how I felt. When she told me she was pregnant, I left. I stayed away five years, but I never could move on. I loved her. So I came back."

"But you couldn't love me?" Holly asked, a cold edge to her voice.

"I tried. You were a good child, no trouble at all, but no."

"Why was mom in the trunk of the car, tied and gagged?"

"She wouldn't stop talking about you. Finally I couldn't listen any longer. I told her we'd go back for you, got her out of the car, hit her, put tape around her hands and shoved her into the trunk. I put tape over her mouth to shut her up. I taped her ankles together. Then I drove on."

"How did you shoot her?"

"I pulled open the hatch in the seat to the trunk. I could see her body. I fired six shots. When they blew my tires, I crashed into a guard rail and ran into the woods. They caught me quickly with dogs. I pled guilty to avoid the death penalty."

"If you loved her, how could you shoot her?"

"Survival instincts. They were on to me. She could witness against me."

After a long silence, Holly asked "Do I have grandparents, aunts, uncles, cousins?"

"My mom is still alive. No one else. She lives in Sacramento, California. Her name is Alice Hollis. She is hurt that her son is in jail for life."

"I'm glad you are in jail for life. My mom was my everything. You took her away from me. I was only five."

He was silent. Certainly not apologetic or remorseful. Holly stood to leave.

"May you suffer each day for having killed my mom, a woman you profess to love. Come on, Dad, we are done here."

After the road trip Holly refocused on school, soccer, and John and me. John played the tape for me and I went from anger at Jim to pride in Holly. She blossomed into maturity. She took charge of her life and planned her future, with law enforcement as her goal.

This trip down memory lane can only be enhanced later today. At 2 pm Holly graduates from high school. John won't be with us in person—he died last year—but I know he looks down with pride at the child of our later years. This child who was put out on a stormy spring night like an unwanted puppy: Holly Martin Patterson.

BRAD G GARBER
DASH NAKED

Dash naked through the verdant forest glade
damp tips of tall grass brushing your skin
cool air rushing into your heaving lungs
and know the senses of the whitetail deer.
Let your bare feet touch the richness of earth
electric pulses of a breathing planet
rising up and into your hungry body
like water rising through the capillaries of trees.
Move beneath dappled woodland sunlight
leaves above you fluttering their shadows
as if to applaud the sensuality of your passing
your camouflage a simple act of boldness.

(cont)

There you may satiate the hunger in your soul
in the connection lost but found again
between what you were and then became
and now release yourself to childhood joys.
Dash naked through the verdant forest glade
gathering bouquets of remembrance and delight
to set upon the sturdy wooden table of your life
like centerpieces of a time well experienced

Garber

GREAT AMERICAN

There goes the Great American
    in the train.
I've known several Great Americans.
There is the physician in a small
        Wisconsin town, who delivered
babies and life-saving procedures
        to thousands of farmers, shop keepers
        fire fighters, children, bankers…
it didn't matter.
There is the fourth-generation farmer
        steeped in earth and cow shit
who struggled, who cared
        for his animals and tradition
and the agricultural mechanism
        that fed his country.
There is the teacher, beloved
        by every young mind, thirsty
for information, understanding, safety
        and mostly love
who was a fortress and friend
        a lighthouse in the storm
a lifelong guide.
There is every mother, every father
        who strove to improve
support, enlighten, strengthen
        every child
who did the best they could do.

There are not enough trains.

Garber

MARTHA K DAVIS
WILD KINGDOM
for Leigh Titus

Four days after her father died, Janet lost driving too.

She panicked at an intersection, surrounded by cars that sped, veered, headed in every direction, following an orderly plan that she no longer understood. She sat paralyzed through three green lights, while the drivers behind her blared their horns and swore at her as they squeezed their cars past. No one sat beside her to tell her what to do.

It was her father who had taught her, many years ago. The summer before her sixteenth birthday, he drove up from the barn in his pickup, calling to her. After she slid behind the steering wheel, he explained how the clutch and the gear shift worked, and kept quiet as she stalled, one, two, three times. "More gas," he suggested. "Ease the clutch out."

Then, like stroking out into the water of a lake, she was gliding forward, gaining momentum, in another element altogether. She took to it as easily as she had learned to swim. They drove down narrow back roads past their neighbors' farms, leaving in their wake tractors carting hay bales and corn. He taught her how to listen to the engine, how to downshift on the hills instead of using the brake. After she earned her license they would climb into the truck and set off into the countryside after supper, her father beside her contemplating the land as Janet navigated the curving asphalt rivers that flowed before her.

When the police arrived at the intersection where she was marooned, one of the officers escorted her in the patrol car to her house in Mission Hills while the other drove her sedan behind them. After that day, whenever she had to leave home, she relied on Don and the occasional bus.

Now, six years later, Janet is losing the ability to sleep. The effects of this loss are harder to gauge. Her limitations sneak up on her at unexpected moments, when, for example, Don asks her a simple question and she can't remember what they have been talking about. She has tried to sleep during the day, but it's impossible. Sleeping pills frighten her. Instead she drinks diet soda until sundown, hoping the sudden absence of caffeine in her system will leave her insensible. She has accustomed herself to its metallic fizzy taste.

So she is acclimating to the night hours. In the dark, after Don has dozed off, Janet lies in bed watching him breathe. Not his face, but his chest. He inhales and exhales steadily, reliably, yet this does nothing to stem her rising anxiety. She turns over and, in as much detail as she can muster, recalls the plots of the police dramas she watched that evening. She reviews important dates in world history, counts out multiplication tables in her head—anything to make her eyelids grow heavy, but she remains miserably alert. Unease presses against her ribs, beats in her throat. Sometime after midnight Janet gives up and walks out to the living room to watch late-night talk shows, obscure black-and-white movies, even soap operas in Spanish and Chinese. The sagas of love and loss, she is learning, are the same in any idiom. Tucked under a blanket on the couch, eyes smarting, she waits for dawn to arrive, for the world to quicken in the illumination of daylight.

Once—only once—she called the hospital. She was certain that her mother was in great pain and nobody was doing anything about it. After leaving her on hold, the night nurse told Janet her mother was sleeping soundly, her vitals weak but steady. Janet doubted he had actually bothered to get up and check. He had probably held the phone in his lap and counted to twenty, then put the receiver back to his ear.

In the weeks that her mother has been hospitalized, Janet hasn't visited as often as she knows she should, but there are good reasons: Don works all week, and the bus route is inconvenient. What's worse, her mother is becoming difficult. Normally a person of few words, Sophia has become garrulous. She is getting strange notions into her head. She has started making ridiculous requests. It's as though her mother has been replaced by some careless, inconsiderate woman Janet has never met before. She has spoken to the doctors at least twice about altering the dosage of her mother's medication, but they insist that she is lucid and comfortable, and that's all they can hope for. Exasperated, Janet is impatient for the day she can take her mother home.

This evening, walking down the hall toward her mother's room, Janet cautions her husband to be cheerful. "And talk to her more, Don," she says, picking a stray thread off the sleeve of his Angels jersey. "Tell her what you told me about the success of your group's newest implant devices. She might be interested. Or something from the paper. They report good news once in a while, don't they?"

"She doesn't want to listen to me, Janet. She wants to be with you."

Janet frowns. "Or tell her that joke you thought was so funny the other day, about the young girl who saw a male dog sniffing a female dog and asked somebody famous what they were doing."

Don's gust of laughter startles her. "It was Noel Coward. 'The one in front has suddenly gone blind, and the other one has very kindly offered to push him.'"

She stops in front of her mother's closed door, smoothing back her hair, barely listening. "That's the one. Just be nice to her. We need to keep her spirits up."

As Don pushes open the heavy door, Janet loses her balance slightly, no doubt light-headed from lack of sleep. Her husband reaches for her arm, but she swats him away. He stands back so she can enter first.

Sophia is sitting upright in the bed, propped by pillows. Her eyes are closed, her hands on the light blanket empty. An IV drips into her arm. At the doorway, Janet sees the wasting away of her mother's body for the first time. What was once solid flesh has turned translucent. Her broad bones seem to have shrunk. Her mother's creased face looks diminished, bruised with illness. The agitation stirs in Janet's chest. She bites her lip hard.

Sophia opens her eyes and smiles. "You've come. Is that Don behind you? Come in, both of you, don't be afraid." Janet goes to her mother, who takes Janet's hands in her own. "Why, you were never hesitant with me before. Is it because I'm dying?"

"Mom, you're not dying. What a thing to say." Janet laughs, glancing back at Don.

"Why, of course I am. Don knows. It's there in his face. You can learn a lot about a person just by looking at his face."

"Speaking of which, did I tell you I'm learning to read palms?" Janet asks. "I read Don's the other night. He's going to have a long life and be very successful, but at some point he'll experience a major tragedy. Oh, and he's got some travel ahead."

"Let's hope it's not back to Florida," Don says, coming to stand beside her.

"I suppose Janet can't be blamed because you have no surprises ahead of you," Sophia tells him.

"I don't know what disaster I have in store," Don points out.

"Don't you?" Sophia asks.

Her tone reminds Janet of her mother's words the night before her and Don's wedding. The two families were in a hotel restaurant, folding their thick cloth napkins as the waiters cleared the large table. Don was standing at the other end of the room, cornered by her uncle who was apparently giving him a bit of advice in private. "He could break your heart," Janet's mother said as they watched him make another futile gesture toward the door, "but I think you're more likely to break his." It was the only observation she ever made about their marriage. Now, almost thirty years later in a hospital room, Janet realizes how little her mother respected Don from the beginning.

Don says, "I'll leave the two of you alone. I'm glad to see you again, Sophia."

Her mother's gaze has wandered. Janet turns to her husband. "I'll be down in about half an hour."

When he has gone, Janet tells her mother, "There's no reason to be rude."

Sophia faces her, blue eyes blazing. "There's no reason you can't visit me by yourself. You don't have to make him come too."

"I can't drive, Mom. You know that. Besides, Don's fine with bringing me. He enjoys waiting in the lobby. He reads."

"You can drive, Janet. You just don't want to."

Janet is finding it hard to breathe. "No. I can't." Gone are the days of roads like rivers.

Chin tipped up, Sophia studies her daughter. "You look terrible. Your eyes are bloodshot, and you've got craters below them. You look like you haven't been outdoors for days. Have you been taking care of yourself?"

"Of course." Janet has told her mother nothing about her recent bout of sleeplessness. There would be no point.

Sophia pats the bed. "Come, sit close to me."

Janet lays her purse on the chair near the door and sits on the edge of her mother's bed, careful not to disturb the fragile body beneath the blanket. Perching there reminds Janet of all the nights her mother came into her bedroom whenever she woke herself up, crying out from bad dreams. Her mother used to sit beside her and stroke her hair. She stayed until Janet fell back asleep. Do you remember, Janet almost asks aloud. She glances at the monitor wire taped to her mother's bony chest beneath her nightgown, the sentence catching in her throat.

"Did you bring them?" her mother asks.

Janet twists around and looks up at the television suspended from the ceiling. It's turned off, as always. She herself paid the extra fee for its use. She can't fathom why her mother doesn't watch it, a distraction to pass the hours. In every other room down the hall, the TV plays all day, the volume either turned up high or muted. Silent or not, at least it is on, an undeniable sign of life.

"Do you remember *Wild Kingdom*?" she asks, still gazing up at the blank screen. In its gray face she can see the exaggerated bulge of her mother's hospital bed, her mother's head a distant balloon. In the corner Janet herself barely registers, a thin, indeterminate shadow. She puts her hand up to her face, looking for the reflected movement. "Last night—this morning, actually—I saw a rerun on the Discovery Channel. About the African plains and the food chain there. Near the end, a lioness tracked a herd of gazelle. They showed everything: her stalking, her attack, the way the herd scattered as one gazelle fell, all except the gazelle's fawn. It just stood there, watching, as the lioness tore into its mother. You could see the animal's neck break, the blood on the lion's jaws. As soon as the mother was dead, the lioness killed the fawn. It didn't even know enough to run away."

Sophia taps Janet's knee. "Did you bring them?" she repeats.

Janet looks back at her mother. Sophia's white hair has thinned, and her scalp shows through in patches. Janet doesn't know which upsets her more, the hair loss or her mother's absurd question. As soon as the hospital releases her, Janet thinks, they'll take a trip. They could go to Africa, where the wildlife now lives on reserves. Or they could go back to Pennsylvania, to see if any of the old farms are still operating.

Janet stands, walks to the door, opens it and peers down the empty hall. She closes the door and leans against it. "Even if I had brought the pills, you know it wouldn't work. They'd only pump your stomach."

"Oh dear."

Janet is astonished by the depth of disappointment in her mother's voice. Then she is angry.

"Mom, they'd know I helped you. I could be arrested. Then where would you be?"

"Why, still here, I suppose." Sophia closes her eyes.

"Are you in pain?" Alarmed, Janet returns to the bed and studies the heart monitor, expecting to see a sharp spike. She looks for the control among the bedclothes to call for help.

"No, no, they keep me doped up pretty well." Her mother gazes up at her. "I sleep a lot. But I'm tired. I'm tired, Janet. I'm ready to go. I hoped you would help me." Sophia passes her hand over the blanket, smoothing the place beside her where Janet was sitting before. "It's only a question of time. I can wait, but I'd prefer to die now."

"Mom, please stop it." Janet puts her hands over her ears. "You're being ridiculous."

"Never mind, never mind." Sophia reaches up to pull her

daughter's arm down. "I won't ask you again."

Janet lets her hands drop. She has heard her mother's weariness, a state she is dimly aware has nothing in common with the vigilant fatigue she herself feels every day, every night. She knows her mother will find some other means. She has always been determined. Her father would have said stubborn. In the past, when her mother felt something needed to be done, she generally found a way to do it herself. To fend off foreclosure, she took over the farm work Janet's father couldn't handle so that they wouldn't have to pay extra wages. Later she left him alone for two months and flew to San Diego to help out when Janet broke her ankle. When Janet's father began his decline, it was her mother who sold the farm and moved the two of them to an assisted-living apartment complex not far from Janet and Don. Now Janet wants her mother to put her formidable will to the service of her own recovery. The doctors have told Janet there is nothing they can do—her mother cannot be cured by medicine or surgery—but she has heard of reversals, and even of full recuperation.

She sits on the bed again, gingerly. "You're feeling low right now. You need something to do. I could bring you your needlepoint. Or would you like some magazines?"

"No, Janet, no more magazines."

"What, then?" Janet asks. Whatever her mother wants, she will ask Don to drive her to buy it.

Sophia says nothing. She brings her hands together in her lap.

"I haven't managed to get over to your apartment this week," Janet says after a moment, picking at the edge of her mother's blanket. "I'm afraid nobody's been looking after your plants."

"Janet." Her mother's voice is gentle. "Take them home with you. Or throw them out."

Janet looks up. "I can't, Mom. They're yours."

Janet stares at her mother. Below her wispy white hair, Sophia's face shines with a soft light Janet has never seen before. It is not the ghastly glow of the disease but something else, a radiance that is entirely her own. Janet looks away from her mother's steady gaze, unnerved.

She says, "That show I was telling you about? I lied. The fawn ran away when it saw the lioness kill its mother. The film team trailed it, and it was adopted by the herd of gazelle. The fawn was saved."

Sophia nods, but Janet can't be sure her mother is listening.

"Mom, you're getting the best care available here. When you're better, we can talk about moving you back home. Now you're tired. It's time for me to leave."

Sophia takes one of Janet's hands in both her own. "I remember that episode."

"What episode?"

"Why, *Wild Kingdom*, of course. Sponsored by Mutual of Omaha. Hosted by Marlon Perkins. It was on Sunday nights."

Her mother has lost none of her memory. She appears to Janet to be more focused and vibrant than ever before, whereas Janet herself is losing crucial abilities, one after the other. "Channel four," she offers.

"Yes." Sophia grips Janet's hand. Afraid, Janet wants to pull away. "There was no fawn, Janet. The lioness attacked one gazelle, and the others escaped across the plains, never looking back. She died alone."

"I need to go, Mom. Don's waiting. He'll be hungry."

Sophia turns her daughter's hand over. She traces a crease in Janet's palm with an unsteady finger. She says, "This is the lifeline, isn't it?"

Janet looks at her mother's shriveled hands. They are the hands of a person who has no surprises ahead of her: not only old but worn out. She remembers Sophia's smooth hands from more than fifty years ago, feeling her forehead for fever, offering aspirin and a cool glass of water, pulling up the blankets so she could fall back asleep.

These are those same hands. How can she let them go?

WILL WALKER
CONSTITUTIONAL

Dreamlike, my new route takes me past
the high school diamond, deserted for summer.
There's a whiff of Fellini in the heavy air—
a busy stillness, the ghost of my youth
drifting by my left hand, then my right.

I walk to the plate and stand as if to hit—
lefty, looking at the field over my right shoulder.
You know how the scenes of your youth
look so small, tiny desks and cramped living rooms?

(cont)

Never so on a diamond. It's always large,
like the proofs of Pythagoras, stretching
green and immense from one foul line
to the other, the place you stand alone,

in shouting distance of your teammates,
on your own. Which is how I peer
at deep center, then lower my gaze
and walk to first, my position, which I fielded
as if my life depended on it. And in a way it did.

Then around the sad plastic bases—stealing second
at a crawl, touching third on the inside corner,
making all the speed I can, digging for home
as if my life depends on it—and it does.
I cross home at a leisurely walk, well ahead
of the throw. Score one for my team. And walk on.

Walker

DAVID JAMES
ARS POETICA: KROGER'S ON GRAND RIVER
for Chloe Maple

I take my granddaughter to the grocery store
to buy dinner; she chooses a chocolate smoothie,
Brie cheese and sea salt pita chips, refusing
the cold shrimp with dipping sauce,
the sushi, the fried chicken.

In the car, parked under a streetlight,
we share chunks of soft cheese with chips
and talk about the day, but mostly
about how good the cheese tastes.

(cont)

I'm not sure her parents would approve
of this dinner,
but I'm a ji-chan and it's my job
to give her a taste of freedom and choice,
within reason, of course.
The joy in her face and voice
is enough to make my heart smile.

And you never know:
this may be her memory of me,
decades from now,
when she walks into a grocery store
to buy something
to eat
with her own granddaughter.

James

HAVA KOHL-RIGGS
WHAT'S EGGS GOT TO DO WITH IT

Last night I decided to cook. I hadn't cooked anything for a long while. My gas bill has been so low that I've considered discontinuing the service to avoid monthly fees. But last night I decided to cook eggs. Hard boiled eggs. At first, I thought two, then three, but settled on six, since, after all, what's the point of only two or three? As long as you're boiling the water for two, you might as well make six. That way, you'll have leftovers. On the internet I found a brilliant recipe for the perfect hard boiled egg. The instructions are to put the uncooked eggs in a saucepan, cover with water and bring to a boil. When the water has boiled, take the saucepan off the heat and let the eggs stand in the hot, just boiled, water for five minutes. The eggs will be perfectly hard boiled, even if you forget and leave them in the pan for hours. It's possible they're only perfect if you take them out of the pan after five minutes as directed. I've never managed that. I invariably forget about the eggs after I remove the pan from the heat.

Last night, I forgot about the eggs *before* removing the pan from the heat. I was engrossed in a book, a fascinating memoir by a woman who'd been divorced twice and married three times and then became friends with her second husband after she married the third one and then he died. It was funny at the same time as it was poignant. Turns out, her third husband, the only one she was happily married to, later has a tragic accident, suffers massive brain damage, and has to live the rest of his life in a nursing home because he's so damaged and sometimes violent with her. She wrote another memoir about that marriage, too, and I knew about that second memoir while reading the first one, so even though *she* didn't know the tragedy awaiting her, *I* did, which leant an even more poignant tone to the book. She loved to cook, and cooked all through her first, second and third marriages as well as the spaces in-between and afterwards. I sort of remembered I was cooking hard boiled eggs when an aromatic scent, like something roasting, floated in to the living room. I was starting to get hungry but still didn't recall I had eggs boiling on the stovetop. Then I heard a popping sound and remembered. Damnit, my eggs are exploding.

    I jumped off the sofa to view the damage but fortunately there was little. I told you, it's a terrific recipe, and nothing can spoil the perfect hard boiled eggs when you follow the instructions, or even if you try to follow them and fail. The eggs had, indeed, exploded. They'd roasted after being boiled. There they were, in the sauce pan, perfect orbs of white with dark brown scorched spots where the eggs met the pan. The explosions had cracked each egg open, revealing the perfectly boiled and roasted eggs within. They were easy to peel, these eggs. and tasted just fine. When I smashed one with a fork, the whites were a bit rubbery, but hard boiled egg whites are always a bit rubbery, don't you think? *I* don't consider this foray into cooking a failure. There are only two eggs remaining in the fridge, and I'll probably eat them tonight.

    When did I stop cooking? My younger son was still living at home but had landed a job at Taco Bell, his favorite restaurant. He started taking all of his meals there—his Mexican co-workers fed each other for free even on days off. I had tired of cooking for my family. My husband avoided the kitchen and had quit doing the dishes following the meals I served him. I was satisfied with salads and tofu or sardines. Eating from the fridge, I called it. Early in our relationship, when he was courting me, he baked bread and cooked stews and gave me the impression that he was a domestic sort of man and that we would share household chores. but he was only putting on an act to reel me in. He stopped cooking after I was hooked, less than three months after our first date, and yet for some strange reason, I believed that the domestic side of him was just hiding because somehow I'd scared it off.

About fifteen years into our marriage, I came into the kitchen and was surprised to find him chopping vegetables for an omelet he was preparing. I was so delighted, I picked up a knife and started chopping, too, thinking I would help and we'd cook together, a dream of intimacy I still harbored. I looked up to find him sitting at the breakfast bar talking with me, but he'd put down his knife and his hands were idle

After we divorced, he wrote to me and asked for the recipe for my kale soup. I understood then that he'd found a new woman to court. I sent him the recipe but left out its secret ingredient, the eggs.

EDWARD RIELLY
A DEPARTURE

The ambulance pulled out, moved
slowly down the driveway, turned right,
disappeared along the gravel road.
My father was the passenger,
at least the body of my father,
his true self, what I had known
beneath the striped bib overalls,
beneath the face unshaven with
a day or two's growth of beard,
beneath the blotched skin of his forehead,
beneath, especially, the thin chest,
was somewhere else. Perhaps still
in the farmhouse with my mother
and older brother, perhaps in some
sort of heaven, deservedly.

I was not there, a few hundred miles
away, but my brother told of watching
the ambulance pull away and swore
that my father, dead then for a couple hours
or so, had lifted up to look out,
a final glance at the farm he had worked
through all our growing up,
the land he had plowed and planted

(cont)

and harvested through the seasons.
I cannot quite believe this, yet not quite
disbelieve it either. Whatever my brother saw
or thought he saw or imagined, it is
all the same: a leaving that would not
be undone, a departure like no other.

Rielly

IAIN MACDONALD
BURN YOUR JOURNAL

Otherwise, they will come to it
in their grief, seeking solace, only
to find, if you have really tried
to reveal your self to yourself,
places where you railed against them
and their claims of love, discover times
when you despised the very life you led.

Those words once served a purpose,
but they are not the ones that should
outlive you. Do everyone a kindness.
Feed the pages to the flames.

GLEN WEISSENBERGER
STOPS ALONG THE WAY

    Kevin Hunter, a veteran passenger on the northernmost branch of the Long Island Rail Road, traveled to New York City five days a week, fifty weeks a year. He boarded the train in the small village of Port Washington, located on the eastern shore of Manhasset Bay, and disembarked at Pennsylvania Station on Manhattan Island. At the end of the workday, the same rail line took him home. about stand

After almost two decades of commuting, Kevin had become acutely attuned to the variety of sounds the train produces as it proceeds along the track, typically stopping at twelve different commuter stations. An electrified, two-track line with a third rail delivering 750 volts of direct current, the Long Island Rail Road operates trains whose stops and starts produce neither the noise nor the commotion of a steam-driven locomotive. The sounds are subtler, with less explosive bursts and more low-pitch groans and squeals. On a typical day, the only particularly loud departure is in Pennsylvania Station, where the tile walls reverberate and magnify the sound. The familiar amalgamation of squeaks, grumbles, and hisses pleasantly signals to passengers who have boarded at Penn Station that they are on their way home.

Even when napping, Kevin could detect the variation in sounds made by a train as it passed over its only grade crossing at Little Neck Parkway or as it traversed the Manhasset Valley Bridge. The bridge, also known as the Manhasset Viaduct, provides a spectacular view of Manhasset Bay—that is, if you're awake and you're sitting on the north side of the train. On his way home, Kevin usually dozed off until the 181-foot-tall trestle created a distinct variation in the sound of the moving train cars. The track on the bridge produced distinct, higher-pitched vibrations, and on windy days, Kevin could even sense the sway of the trestle. Invariably, when the railway cars passed over the viaduct, he would awaken from his nap, then read *The Wall Street Journal* as the train progressed to its ultimate destination in Port Washington, located about twenty miles from Pennsylvania Station.

Manhasset Bay occupies a unique place in American literature as the fictionalized body of water that separates East Egg and West Egg, as well as Daisy and Gatsby, in F. Scott Fitzgerald's *The Great Gatsby*. As for the Long Island Rail Road, it is embedded in legal culture in the fabled case of Palsgraf v. Long Island Rail Road Co., which is taught to every student in United States law schools. The majority decision, elegantly written by Judge Benjamin N. Cardozo, is considered one of the finest pieces of judicial literature. But neither of these stories has anything to do with Kevin Hunter.

On this particular Wednesday evening in April, Kevin boarded the 6:07 train in Pennsylvania Station, determined not to doze off. Remaining awake would normally be a challenge, but on this day, Kevin had a very good reason to stay alert. He had followed a woman onto the third car with the hope of meeting her.

When Kevin first saw the woman waiting on the platform in Penn

Station, he felt a curious attraction. Unquestionably handsome, she had an amicable air of self-confidence. She was, however, a woman of Kevin's age, at least that was his estimation, and Kevin typically found women at least ten years younger more to his liking. Nevertheless, the woman initially evoked feelings of a comfortable affection, the type a man might feel for a distant cousin. But his feelings became more complex and more enigmatic as he waited to board the train. Kevin even experienced a whimsical sense of intrigue in trailing her into the third car.

    The woman selected a window seat on the left side of the train car, but a male commuter immediately sat next to her. Disappointed, Kevin took a seat across the aisle. After the man disembarked at Bayside, however, Kevin found he could surreptitiously study the woman's profile from his current position, and he was pleased by what he saw. Momentarily, he considered relocating to the seat next to her and, perhaps, initiating a conversation. Just as he was about to stand up, however, the woman answered a call on her cell phone. *Probably for the best*, thought Kevin. He did not want to appear awkward, or even worse, sinister.

    Making the best use of the camouflage provided by his newspaper, Kevin furtively glanced across the aisle. He found if he held his head facing the paper, then moved his eyes completely to the left, he could catch a reasonably clear view of the woman. She possessed a professional deportment with conservative clothing well exceeding department store quality. Her head nodded in reaction to the cell phone caller. *Likely speaking with her husband*, thought Kevin. Her left hand faced the window, and Kevin found it impossible to discern whether she was wearing a wedding ring. But her right wrist was adorned by a tennis bracelet with brilliant diamonds that gleamed in the dim light of the railroad car.

    Just when Kevin felt he had gathered all of the intelligence about the woman he possibly could, the train slowed its speed and the air brakes hissed in anticipation of arriving at the Great Neck Station. Several commuters, aroused by the sound of the brakes, stood up, and started walking toward the doors—among them, the woman who strangely captivated Kevin. As she made her way toward the front of the train, Kevin lowered his newspaper. The unsteadiness of the moving railroad car did not provide a sufficiently stable surface for Kevin to fully assess her gait, but her ambulation was sufficiently captivating to spark a spontaneous smile on Kevin's face.

    As the train pulled out of the Great Neck Station, Kevin told himself he would probably never see the woman again. In New York, a man might notice many attractive women without the materialization of an opportunity to meet. He wrote this off as a missed opportunity, one of many. In different circumstances, Kevin might see an interesting woman, then maneuver to meet her. It could happen waiting in line for coffee, sitting at a lunch counter, or shopping for groceries. He was divorced, and his vigilance was commonplace for a man in his situation. Well practiced in the art of the casual encounter, he appreciated that meeting an unfamiliar woman should never appear to be the product of prowling or stalking. The so-called "chance meeting," mastered by both genders, and potentially initiated by either, enjoyed a robust and established practice in New York City.

The next day, Kevin hadn't given a thought to the woman who had commanded his attention on the platform in Pennsylvania Station, that is, until he arrived just on time to catch the 6:07 to Port Washington. He suddenly remembered. With no opportunity to survey the crowd of people already in the process of boarding the train, Kevin positioned himself to enter the third car. Once inside, he found no trace of the woman he saw yesterday. With the choice of sitting beside several men and women who occupied the window seats, he quite naturally selected a seat next to a woman. Opening *The Wall Street Journal*, his eyes drifted to the left hand of the woman beside him. It held a cell phone and displayed a princess cut diamond on the ring finger. He folded his newspaper and fell asleep.

Three weeks passed and Kevin all but forgot about the woman who once intrigued him on the platform in Pennsylvania Station. During that time, he met Darlene Cunningham, who impatiently waited ahead of him in line at Starbucks in pursuit of a latte. He initiated a conversation, then invited her to lunch, at which time he learned she was an associate in a large law firm and consumed with becoming a partner. While sufficiently prepossessing to warrant Kevin's interest, her earnest striving to achieve partnership gave her an overstressed aura and a preoccupied demeanor. She also lived in New Jersey, a logistical deal breaker.

Then, on a Thursday evening as Kevin approached the fourth car of the 6:07 in Pennsylvania Station, he noticed his mystery woman as she boarded the third car. Allowing other commuters to pass around him, he stepped back, then headed for the third car. Experiencing a feeling of modest euphoria when he noticed she took a window seat, he nevertheless hesitated to sit next to her until the car was reasonably filled. It then became a matter of strategic timing, lingering at the back of the car until most of the window seats were occupied, then dashing to claim the prize of the seat next to her. As far as he could tell, Kevin gave the impression that his seat selection was a matter of random happenstance. Anything else could get things off to bad start.

As he sat down, the woman turned to him with a polite smile that grew into something more inviting. He smiled back in equal measure and opened his *Wall Street Journal.* As the woman picked up her cell phone, Kevin began reading his newspaper, recognizing that the time to commence a conversation would not be until the distracting sounds of the departure from Pennsylvania Station were behind them.

At about the time the train emerged from the East River Tunnel, Kevin turned to the woman. It was the slightest movement, but he calculated she might notice him.

"Kevin," the woman volunteered. "Kevin Hunter. Right?"

Initially astonished, then self-consciously embarrassed, Kevin replied, "Why yes. But you have me at a disadvantage."

"Disadvantage?"

"It's an expression—probably outdated. I mean, I can't place you." In that instant, Kevin thought the word disadvantage was particularly apt. "You look familiar, but—"

The woman cocked her head demurely. "I'm Regina Turlington. You probably knew me as, Gina."

"Yes, the name is familiar." Kevin was lying.

Gina licked her lips. "You don't remember our kiss?"

Kevin felt the capillaries in his neck distending. "This must've been a long time ago, because in all truthfulness, I don't remember." He really had no choice but to be honest.

Gina pushed her auburn hair over her shoulder, apparently finding some pleasure in having Kevin, as he put it himself, at a disadvantage. "Well, it really wasn't a romantic kiss. It just was supposed to look that way."

Kevin meticulously folded *The Wall Street Journal* into quarters, a process that gave him a few moments to think. Still baffled, he confessed, "I'm sorry, but I just don't really recall." Then smiling and regaining a substantial portion of his composure, "You'll have to give me some hints. It's not like me to forget a kiss." His smile became broader. "Come on, just a few hints."

Placing her phone in her lap, Gina's face became pensive as if she was really thinking up clues. "It was in high school."

With that single fact, Kevin began detecting a growing sense of elation. Then, a feeling not unlike a chill ran up his spine and into his neck. "High school? We dated in high school?"

Gina obviously relished having the advantage. "No. We didn't date. You never asked me out." She facetiously pouted.

At that moment, the train emerged from the underground portion of its journey into the twilight of the early evening. It would soon be approaching the Flushing Main Street Station.

Gina's phone rang, or more accurately, it melodiously chimed the introductory bars of Beethoven's Fifth Symphony. Answering it, she spoke in a muffled tone to the caller for a few minutes. Then, covering the phone, she whispered to Kevin, "It's my mother. This will take a while."

Kevin sat patiently, at least until the train stopped at Little Neck Station. He knew the next station was Great Neck, where Gina exited the first time he saw her. More anxious than seemingly warranted, Kevin tore a corner off of *The Wall Street Journal* and wrote on it with a gold Cross pen produced from his shirt pocket, "I need more hints." He passed it to Gina.

As the air brakes sounded for the approach to Great Neck, Gina looked at the note, said goodbye to her mother, and stood up.

Kevin stepped out into the aisle with a searching look on his face.

As Gina brushed past him, she whispered, "I'll be on the same train tomorrow. Third car." She smiled winsomely and exited the train.

Kevin began to understand why he felt a warm attraction to Gina when she was simply a mysterious woman standing on the platform waiting to board the 6:07 in Pennsylvania Station. She was a woman with whom he had some history. A latent familiarity, previously at work in his subconscious, started blossoming into a palpable sense of rapport. The affinity quickly grew into infatuation. By the time the train reached its final destination in Port Washington, Kevin sensed an excitement he hadn't felt since he went to his senior prom with a black-haired girl whose name was Angelina. After the dance, they went to her house and kissed for hours in the unfinished basement on a decaying sofa—just as she had promised.

When he arrived at his home in Sands Point, just north of Port Washington, rather than making himself his usual scotch, he immediately ran to the basement where boxes were neatly stored on metal shelves. He removed the box labeled "Senior year, high school" and found the largest book in the container. It was his high school yearbook, and he immediately turned to the index to search for Regina Turlington. He scanned all of the students whose name began with T, but he found nothing. Flipping through the pictures in the front of the yearbook, again no results. There was no Gina Turlington anywhere to be found in his yearbook. He would have to wait until tomorrow to learn more about their kiss.

The next day, Kevin really should have remained at his office until late in the evening to review projects from junior associates, but he was too consumed with anticipation. He had sufficient tenure in his firm to set his own deadlines, and certainly the projects could wait a day or two, even if they involved millions of dollars. Before leaving, he went to the executive washroom, where he encountered Arthur Morrison, who started at the firm with him eighteen years ago.

"Kevin, you look rather happy," observed Arthur as he splashed water on his face, standing in front of the mirror next to Kevin. "I know that look. You must have a date tonight."

Kevin smiled into the mirror as he brushed the sides of his hair with his fingertips. "Not really a date. Actually, it seems better. I'm meeting a woman I knew in high school."

Arthur shook his wet hands into the sink. "Tell me about her." He began drying his hands with paper towels he pulled from the dispenser.

"Well, I met her on the train. I felt a certain attraction to her, but at first, I didn't understand why. Then when we talked, she told me we knew each other in high school."

Straightening his tie in the mirror, Arthur inquired, "Did you date in high school?"

"Here's the strange part," said Kevin, shaking his head. "She said we didn't date, but, according to her, I kissed her. I don't specifically remember her, but I do have this feeling of infatuation. She didn't look like the kind of person who would make up a story just to have a conversation with me. I must have known her, because the feeling is much stronger than simply an initial attraction."

Arthur balled up the paper towels he used to dry his face and threw them in the trash. As he walked toward the door, he called out, "Good luck, Kevin. It's about time you met somebody who gives you those kinds of feelings."

Kevin stood on the platform waiting to board the 6:07. As the train approached its time to depart, Kevin looked around with a slight sense of panic. There was no sign of Gina. Did she board the train without him noticing it? He tried to conjure up her face in his mind and discovered it was something of a challenge. But she had distinctive auburn hair. He couldn't have missed that. He entered the third car and walked up and down the aisle searching for Gina's face. She was not on the third car. He reluctantly took an aisle seat and contemplated whether there had been a mistake—a possible miscommunication as to the plan. Ultimately, he decided that Gina was simply not interested in meeting him. He had experienced rejection from women before, but never after such an auspicious beginning. He considered the possibility, however, that their conversation yesterday on the train might have been a sequel to an unpleasant experience when Gina knew him in high school. Perhaps he callously rejected her without recognizing her interest. But he kissed her—at least that's what she told him. He unfolded his *Wall Street Journal* and began to read.

As the 6:07 pulled into the Great Neck Station, Kevin looked out the window at the passengers disembarking onto the platform. He failed to see any woman with auburn hair. But then, his vantage point was limited. He resigned himself to his disappointment and resumed reading the newspaper as the train departed.

Suddenly, there was a tap on his shoulder, and Kevin looked up to see Gina's face, his recognition confirmed by her auburn hair.

"May I sit down?" It really wasn't a question because Gina sat immediately next to Kevin. "I'm sorry I didn't meet you on the train when it left Penn Station. I forgot that I wasn't working in the city today. I didn't want to disappoint you or appear to be rude, so I boarded the train in Great Neck. You know, where I live. So, here I am." A thin smile appeared on her face, and she put her shoulders back as if to present herself.

Kevin smiled agreeably. "This is a pleasant surprise."

"Normally, I would have just waited until we met again on the train, but I'm going to be out of town all of next week. I just didn't want you to think I was avoiding you." Gina's cell phone chimed the opening measure of Beethoven's Fifth Symphony. She looked at the phone and said, "It's my mother."

Kevin tried his best to suppress a grimace.

"Don't worry," said Gina pushing a key on her phone. "I'll call her back. But actually, we don't have much time."

"You're not dying, are you?" It was the first thing that came to Kevin's mind.

Gina laughed out loud. "No, I'm quite well. I mean that we don't have much time for this conversation. I just got on the train to tell you that I would be gone for a week. I'm getting off at Manhasset and taking the next train back to Great Neck."

"That gives us only a few minutes," said Kevin plaintively.

"Better than you thinking me a rude person." She cleared her throat. "I didn't want that."

"Well, then, perhaps we should dispense with the clues, and you should tell me about our high school days. You know, I looked for you in my yearbook, and I couldn't find you."

Gina put her phone in her purse and turned in her seat to look directly at Kevin. "That's because I graduated a year before you. Our kiss occurred when I was a senior and you were a junior."

Now Kevin became even more mystified. Kissing an older woman—he should definitely remember that.

"Oh, my gosh," declared Gina. "The train is already starting to slow down. Meet me a week from Monday for the 6:07 on the platform. I'll try to explain everything then." She got up, stood by the door, and when it opened, she coyly waved goodbye. Gina vanished to be gone for over a week.

When Kevin arrived home, he once again returned to the basement. He found the container marked "Junior year, high school." In the box he found the yearbook. He flipped through the pages and almost immediately found Gina's senior photograph. Graduation pictures are supposed to be flattering, employing the photographer's best techniques to present the subject as attractively as possible. In the case of Gina, the photographer fell short of his mark. While it would be inaccurate to say that Gina looked homely, the best that could be said is that she appeared quite ordinary.

He checked the index. Gina's picture could also be found on the pages devoted to girls' field hockey, the honor society, and the drama club. Now he was beginning to remember. He found the pictures on the drama club page, and in one picture, there he was, standing next to Gina in all of her ordinariness.

During the ensuing week, Kevin looked at Gina's yearbook pictures repeatedly. Each time he studied the photographs, he developed increasing anticipation of meeting her again. Each of the pictures intrigued him, and even though her graduation picture was not entirely flattering, Kevin found her other photographs scattered through the yearbook to be quite charming. She was slender, almost statuesque, and she had a knack for posing in a playfully provocative manner. A picture on the drama club page with her face in full stage makeup Kevin found particularly captivating.

As the week progressed, Kevin breezed through his work,

actually moving up the closing dates on several of his projects. His associate, Arthur Morrison, commented more than once that Kevin appeared to be in a splendid mood.

"It must be this new woman in your life," suggested Arthur.

"Well, she's not in my life—yet. But we're meeting again on Monday." With a wistful smile, Kevin continued, "It's not really a date. We're just meeting on the train. But I plan to ask her out to dinner. You know, Arthur, it's been a long time since a woman has made me feel this way. I truly sense a strong connection with her already." Kevin didn't disclose to his friend his repeated studying of Gina's playfully provocative pictures in the yearbook.

On the agreed upon Monday, Kevin arrived early on the platform in Pennsylvania Station to wait for the 6:07 train. Shortly after six o'clock, he found himself becoming anxious. Pacing up and down the platform, he looked searchingly for a tall woman with auburn hair. Just when he was about to give up, he was approached by a shapely, blonde woman, probably in her late twenties.

"Excuse me," said the blonde woman, out of breath from running across the platform. "Are you Kevin Hunter?"

"Why, yes."

"I'm Natalie Norton. I work for Gina Turlington. You certainly fit the description. Otherwise, I would've never been able to pick you out among all these other guys. Anyway, she sent me to tell you she's very sorry, but she has to work late tonight. Can you meet her tomorrow?"

"Here on the platform? For the 6:07?"

"Yes. She'll meet you then." Natalie turned briskly, leaving Kevin with only the sight of her long, flowing blonde hair cascading down the back of her neck and onto her shoulders.

Disappointed, Kevin boarded the train, selected a window seat, and began his nap. As the train traversed the Manhasset Viaduct, the unique vibrations awakened him. He unfolded his newspaper and glanced at the person seated next to him, a young woman of no more than twenty scrolling through texts on her cell phone. She possessed the same plainness that Gina exhibited in her graduation picture, and he felt like telling her not to worry, she would blossom into a beauty one day. Of course, he didn't speak to her at all. If he had been motivated to say anything, it would have been to suggest that her appearance might be greatly improved by the removal of the nose ring.

Tuesday evening at six o'clock, Kevin arrived at Pennsylvania Station and ran to the platform for the Port Washington line. Gina was waiting, wearing a navy, double-breasted, pinstripe suit and a striking designer scarf. Along with meticulously applied makeup, she looked like a model in a fashion magazine. Not one of the waif-like creatures, but a more mature model, perhaps for antiaging cream. Kevin walked up to her with a smile and was about to hug her, but he stopped. Her body language wasn't receptive.

Boarding the 6:07 together, Gina took the window seat and began speaking immediately. "Kevin, I'm dreadfully sorry I had to cancel last night. People came in from London unexpectedly. I had to take them out to dinner. They were so jet-lagged that after a few drinks, they were hilariously funny. The Brits are so much more enjoyable than the Germans I have to deal with. The Spaniards are the best. The funniest damn people I've ever met. Full of life."

Kevin turned to face her. "What do you do? It sounds fascinating."

Gina opened her purse, reached in, and removed her cell phone to switch it to silent mode. "When my mother knows I'm on this train, she always calls me. It is true that, with my schedule, riding on the train is the only time I really sit in one place long enough for a conversation. What do I do? My occupation?"

Kevin nodded.

"I own a boutique women's clothing store in the West End. You know, London. I primarily work out of an office in New York City, but really, I could live anywhere on the globe. I'm always traveling."

A clever smile materialized on Kevin's face. "That seems to be the perfect profession for Juliette."

Gina gasped slightly. "You remember!"

Kevin sat back slightly in an effort to strike a theatrical pose. "Yes. I remember gagging you with a scarf. And I recall kissing you, right after you said, 'I love you.'"

"Then you said, 'Juliette, it's goodbye to your tranquility.'" Gina laughed out loud. "But my best line was directed to Lord Edgard and Lady Hurf: 'I'm not ashamed! You can say anything you like, I'll never be ashamed! I love him. I want him for my lover, since you will never let him be my husband. Look. I'm going to kiss him now in front of you.'" The lines were delivered with an artistic gusto rarely heard in a Long Island Rail Road car.

Kevin responded in kind: "'I love you, Juliette.'"

Throwing herself completely into the experience, Gina responded, "I even remember Lady Hurf's lines: 'He is adorable. Look at the breeding in that profile. The exquisite shyness and yet the strength of it. He will make a fairytale husband for our terrible, gentle Juliette.' But when she's reminded that you're a thief, she exclaimed, 'Well, then. It's out of the question. You must go at once!'"

They both laughed, almost uncontrollably.

Kevin had laughed so hard his eyes began to tear. He reached into his back pocket and withdrew a linen handkerchief. "*Thieves' Carnival*, by some French author," he exclaimed.

"Anouilh," interjected Gina. "Jean Anouilh. Almost every high school does the play. I had such a crush on you after you kissed me on stage. But you were more interested in Madeleine McCarthy. You know, the sophomore who did your makeup for the play."

Actually, Kevin had no recollection of why he didn't become involved with Gina in high school. He did recall, however, that he kissed her at least twice in the play, and it was sensational. "Honestly, Gina, I don't know why I didn't ask you out. You were a year older than me. Maybe I was intimidated."

Frowning slightly, Gina replied, "But you dated Jennifer Newberry, and she was in my class."

Kevin vividly recalled the stunning Jennifer Newberry and her rather lifeless, icy kisses. "Then, I have no excuse. But I'll make up for it. Can I take you to dinner?" He felt a palpable chemistry with Gina. "That is, of course, if you're not involved with someone."

The train began making its stop at Bayside. Gina waited until the sound of the air brakes subsided. "No, Kevin, I'm not involved with anyone. But you see, I'm really too busy to date right now. I've just decided not to. I'm traveling all the time—"

"No need to explain. I understand. My work keeps me quite busy as well." Dejection all but swallowed up Kevin Hunter. Days of anticipation suddenly felt like complete foolishness—a waste of resources like losing a substantial amount of cash at a crooked carnival booth.

"What do you do?" asked Gina.

"Real estate." Actually, the detail of Kevin's career as a real estate developer would be impressive to any savvy New Yorker, but there was no need to brandish his dossier now.

Great Neck was only one stop away, and Kevin did his best to fill in the time with meaningless conversation about their mutual classmates. The sound of air brakes ultimately made the final fragments of their exchange unintelligible.

When the train stopped at the Great Neck Station, Kevin stood to allow Gina to exit.

She turned to face him. "I really don't date."

It was meant as a reassurance, but it had no uplifting effect. Kevin smiled and nodded.

Gina reached into her purse and removed a folded piece of paper. "My assistant, Natalie, you met her on the platform yesterday. She wanted me to give this to you. She said she's looking to meet men like you. It's her telephone number." She gave Kevin a forced, cousinly hug, then disappeared from the train.

Three weeks later, Kevin found the folded piece of paper in his suit pocket. As hard as he tried, he could not remember where it came from.

STEVEN PELCMAN
ON THE TENTH ANNIVERSARY OF A HUSBAND'S DEATH

She kneels across the headstone
with both arms resting on top
and her head down
quietly sobbing for
a lover's memory
now etched in stone

but here in a granite reflection
sand and grass are as tender
as skin and carved words replace
the wrinkles he had worn and the smile
he would flash each time they held
each other, and when she picks the weeds

and clears away the pebbles saying
'the wind and the rain have more of him
than I do' she so easily becomes a housewife,
even here in the shade of Florida
trees that take forever to grow, she leans
over a bed half slept in and remembers.

Pelcman

NEIGHBORS

They were newspaper neighbors
sharing the paper every day
to save money, with her
buying it, leaving it at his door

then after reading he returns it
to her door, both of the them retired,
old and always at home with no family to learn
about what is going on in the world.

Her door cracks open to the cold air
in the building's second floor
where the light tells the time of day
and the quiet footsteps to the apartment

across the hall in an excited anticipation
of quickly returning to hear the other
apartment door open and the shuffling
sound of newspaper crunching in an old man's hands.

They rarely spoke or shared what they had read
but they understood the meaning of silence and hope
in the words not spoken and could feel the importance
of which articles meant more by the smudges of
fingerprints that rubbed out a letter or a word
here and there to see who cared about what
in their lives in the dead of winter
as snow swirls and cold air beats against their windows.

Oddly, Wednesday's paper sat motionless
on the welcome mat gathering dust on Thursday
leaving her wondering and worrying if he had somehow
forgotten as his memory had seemed to drift away lately.

He often forgot what day it was and would sometimes
ask if the paper was new or the old one confusing the
old woman and making her feel afraid seeing her own
pain in his sad eyes.

(cont)

On Friday, the paper now weathered and kicked about
by children running upstairs, she attempted to open
the door and called the police who entered the apartment
to find the old man dead and curled against the cold wood.

The old woman blamed herself for not saving him,
for not calling the police the day before and when she
bought the paper on Monday only to see his name and death
listed, she left the paper at his door to ease the loneliness

of an old man's sorrow so that he would not be
forgotten and somehow lost in the memory
of an old building with old people who leave their lives
on welcome mats in the early hours of every day.

Pelcman

LINDSEY ANDERSON
ACADIA

  From the bay window on the east end of the lobby, Evie could watch the late summer sun sink through the sky. When the last rays of dying light slanted across the pine-strewn summit of Cadillac Mountain, the tourists visiting the park that day would pack up their picnics, pile into their station wagons, and drive into town.
  She didn't dislike the tourists. They were, after all, the reason she had a job. But she hated the familiar faces she found among them. Last month a former classmate waylaid her in the canned goods aisle of the grocery store and wanted to know why she hadn't been making contributions to the Dartmouth alumni fund. A few weeks ago, an old professor spotted her at the beach, while she was helping her ten-year-old son, Oscar, sort his collection of seashells by size and color. And just yesterday, Frankie had sauntered, unannounced, into the bed and breakfast where she worked.
  The White Whale had been a fixture of Bar Harbor since the 1920s, when an enterprising fisherman founded an inn above the only speakeasy in the county. Evie had been working there for six years. She

was now an assistant manager and could usually talk about her job around town without a twinge of embarrassment. But whenever Frankie stepped into the lobby of the inn and lifted his sea-glass green eyes to her sandbar brown ones, she wanted to fling her plastic name tag across the room and pretend she was a guest, in town for a weekend of hiking or whale watching. Pretending would have been pointless, though. Frankie's lawyers knew where she worked and how much she earned each year, which meant he knew too.

"Evie," he said, sidling over to her. "You look good."

They'd met at Dartmouth, in a basement bar not far from campus. She'd spilled some of her scotch onto the tops of her loafers and, grinning, he'd told her that she had to dance with him to atone for the sin of wasting decent liquor. She'd known as soon as she placed her hand in his and tried to match his toothy grin with one of her own that she'd be going home with him that evening. What she didn't know then, of course, was that she'd spend the next nine years of her life chasing that crooked smile. She didn't know that she'd turn down a two-year stint in the Peace Corps to live with him in a dilapidated house off the coast of Deer Isle— far from any of her friends—and spend all her free time helping him build an ecotourism company. She didn't, couldn't, know then that she'd come home one gray November day, not long after Greener Pastures had finally started making money, to find that he'd left a stack of divorce papers on their coffee table. But whenever she remembered how he used to kiss her back to life in the early mornings and tell her—sun streaming between their bedroom blinds—that he'd never get tired of waking up beside her, how they used to mark up a map with all the places they'd go when they had more money and time, she wondered if she could have avoided loving him even if she'd known.

"What are you doing here, Frankie?"

"I had a meeting in Portland, figured I'd drive up for the weekend and maybe take Oscar out to dinner, and you too, if you're free. It's been more than a month, Evie."

"It's been two and a half months, actually." Frankie was traveling wherever and whenever he wanted now, and her own world had shrunk to the distance she drove between The White Whale, the front gates of Saint Catherine's School for Children with Special Needs, and the single-story bungalow she bought in Ellsworth last year. "And I've got chili in a crock pot at home."

"It'll keep. The oysters I saw being shucked at Sebastian's on my way here won't, though. Come on, Evie."

Eating oysters with someone who had cut her out of his life as neatly as she clipped coupons seemed like a bad idea. But Oscar liked to see the two of them together, and she hadn't been out to eat in ages. "All right," she agreed, finally. "If he's feeling up to it."

"I'll be at the Bayview, if you need to get in touch with me in the meantime."

"That's silly. You should stay here."

"I don't want to get in your way," Frankie said, looking up at her from his sandbar brown lashes.

"You won't," Evie insisted. "Just give me a second to ring you up."

Not long after Evie led Frankie to his room and promised to meet him at Sebastian's, Baxter walked into the inn.

Baxter was the only homeless man who lived in Bar Harbor year-round. Evie watched him climb up and down the hills of Acadia in the wind and the rain and the cold, dragging branches as wide as flag poles or pieces of sailcloth behind him. He usually wandered into the White Whale shortly before Evie's shift ended, for a cup of coffee and whatever was left of the day's continental breakfast. Sometimes one of the guests would complain about his scruffy appearance, and he'd eat in the alley behind the inn. But usually the guests were more perplexed than perturbed by his tatty clothes, and Evie could let him sit by the fireplace while he ate.

On those afternoons, he'd tell Evie between mouthfuls of muffin or coffee cake about the boat he'd been working on for at least a year, insisting that he'd soon be setting sail for the warm waters of the South Pacific, to places where the beaches were white sand, not black rock, and you could walk barefoot even in February without getting frostbite.

"It'll be ready tomorrow or the day after for sure," he told her again.

"Oh yeah?" Evie was barely listening. She was wondering whether she should change for dinner. There was a cobalt blue cocktail dress in the back of her closet that she'd been wanting to wear, but Frankie would notice if she changed and probably guess that she wanted to impress him.

"I just need another bolt of fabric or two to finish off the sail," Baxter continued. "You think you might have any old bed sheets you don't need anymore?"

The clock was striking five, signaling the end of her shift and her cue to pick Oscar up from chess club. She would have about an hour to get ready once she got home. "All right," she said. "Ask Martha to grab some from the laundry on your way out."

*****

Oscar's elementary school was on the western edge of the island, protected from prying eyes by a phalanx of pine trees. She was a little late that day, and she'd assumed that Oscar would be outside waiting for her when she arrived, but she couldn't see him. He wasn't with Sam, the shy boy with a shock of curly red hair who was his only real friend at school, and he wasn't waiting with Mr. Green either.

When Oscar finally emerged from the building, most of the other students had already disappeared into their parents' cars. Evie could tell from the set of his shoulders that he was upset. But she knew that he wouldn't want her to make a fuss, so she waited until he tossed his backpack into the trunk of her car and settled into his seat to ask about his day.

"I had another accident," he muttered. "Everyone saw."

"I'm sure they understand," Evie said, noting that the baggy jeans hanging from his slender frame weren't his. "You're not the only one at school who has seizures."

"Lewis called me a freak."

"Ben Lewis is a bully."

Oscar pulled his headphones from the backpack and jammed them over his ears, effectively ending the conversation. She drove the rest of the way home in silence, waiting until he was settled in his room with his blanket and a stack of comic books to tell him that Frankie had stopped by the inn that day and wanted to take them out to dinner.

"No," Oscar said simply.

"No?"

"I'm not going."

"He's your father. He wants to see you."

"Then he shouldn't live so far away."

Evie moved a couple of the comic books aside, so that she could sit on the edge of Oscar's bed, and pressed his tiny hand between hers. "He's only in town for a few days."

"Good." Oscar pulled his hand away and reached for one of the comics. "Then I won't have to see him at all."

Evie watched him read for a moment before padding into her bedroom to phone Frankie. "I'm sorry, but he had a bad day at school and just isn't feeling up to dinner tonight."

"I could bring a pizza over there, if he'd rather stay in."

"I think he wants to be left alone for a while, to be honest."

"I see," Frankie said softly. Evie didn't need to see him to know that he was tugging at the fine hairs near the nape of his neck, the way he did whenever he was upset.

"Maybe we can try again tomorrow, if you're still free."

"Hey," he said suddenly. "Why don't you come out to dinner with me anyway? I've already booked the reservation."

"Just the two of us, you mean?"

"Why not?"

She could think of at least a dozen reasons to turn Frankie down. But she'd never been any good at saying no to men, and there was always something in Frankie worth saying yes to. The easy laugh and long eyelashes. The omelets he made on Sunday mornings. The hundreds of "I love you"s he'd mumbled into her ears over the years. It had been a long time since she'd heard one of those.

"I'll see if Karen can babysit."

*****

Dinner with Frankie was going surprising well. The restaurant was quiet, and the wine good. They talked about Greener Pastures over their first glass of wine. She admitted to him over their second that she'd been toying with the idea of opening a business of her own, a bed and breakfast near her sister's home in Norfolk, Virginia—she's stayed there for a few months after the divorce, while her parents looked after Oscar, and dreamt of going back.

"You should do it," Frankie told her.

"Running an inn is different than owning one, though."

"Not that different. And you helped me get Greener Pastures off the ground. That counts as experience too."

"Oscar probably wouldn't like it there."

"He might, though. And I could look after him more. You'd be a lot closer to Baltimore."

"Maybe," Evie allowed. Maybe she'd let Frankie be the responsible one for a change, the practical one, and she'd let herself do something a little impulsive.

She drained a third glass of wine while Frankie ordered them a slice of chocolate cake. And when he invited her back to his room, on the pretense that his air conditioner wasn't working properly and maybe she ought to check it out, she only hesitated a moment before agreeing.

"I like what you've been doing with your hair," he told her as he fumbled with the key to his room. "It suits you."

"Thanks," Evie said, taking the key from his hand and turning it in the lock. "And I like what you're doing with yours too. Even if I'm a little sad to see you don't wear that old flannel jacket everywhere you go anymore."

Once inside, they poured themselves more wine from the bottle in the mini bar—the air conditioner already forgotten—and sat, side by side, on the king-sized bed that filled most of the room. Frankie let one of his hands rest lightly on the mattress, inches from Evie's thigh.

"Remember the weekend we spent in Acadia our first year in Maine?" he asked suddenly. "We had to sleep along the side of the road, because all of the cabins in the park were booked, and there was no way we could have afforded a place like this."

"I remember." They'd spread out their sleeping bags along a soft stretch of grass near the southeast entrance of the park grounds. "I bet you that there were more than a thousand stars in the sky that night, but we only managed to count a couple hundred before we fell asleep."

"We didn't fall asleep. We just got a little distracted," Frankie said, edging his hand closer to her leg.

"That's right. I think we got distracted a couple of times that night, actually." She reached across him to pour herself another glass of wine, and he suddenly leaned toward her and pressed his lips against hers. They were just as warm and as soft as they'd been that night in Acadia so many years ago, before they got married, before she got pregnant, before he left. She remembered that when they woke up the morning after their evening under the stars their faces were wet with dew and their bodies were dotted with constellations of bug bites every bit as impressive as the ones they'd been counting the night before.

Frankie was attempting to unhook her bra when her phone rang. It was the sitter, Karen. "I'm really sorry, Ms. Robichaud, but Oscar's having another seizure. A small one, but still. I think maybe you need to come home.

Evie swore softly and told Karen she'd be right there.

"What's wrong?" Frankie asked, still stroking her back hopefully.

"Oscar needs me. I've got to go."

"I can pull my car around."

"I'll take a cab. See you later, Frankie."

*****

Evie let herself into the lobby of the White Whale a little earlier than normal the next morning. She'd kept Oscar home from school to rest, and she wanted to finish as much as she could at the inn before he woke up, in case she needed to head home again to look after him. She actually liked waking up early anyway. She liked sitting alone in the lobby of the inn, where she could watch the newly risen sun struggling to warm the frigid waters of the Atlantic. Frankie used to tell her while they were living on Deer Isle that the sun lit up the mountains of the Maine coast before it hit any other part of the country, that it rose for them first.

Frankie talked like a poet. He spoke in pretty turns of phrase. But he had too many hopelessly romantic ideas in his head to ever settle for the reality of life with a thirty-four year old woman whose son would probably always need her a little more than he did, who would always have to choose practicality over romance.

By the time the first guests were waking up and wandering down to the lobby for fresh fruit or one of the blueberry muffins Martha had baked the night before, Evie had decided that, if Frankie asked her to spend another evening with him, she would say no. She'd be better off not getting involved with someone who lived so far away, someone who would never be able to understand that the world wasn't all stars and sunshine and trips to Europe, that sometimes a person had to make tough choices, do what they had to instead of what they wanted to do. Her life wasn't a sonnet, and she shouldn't expect some sort of fairytale ending for herself in Virginia.

She poured herself a cup of coffee and walked over to the bay window, where she could stare at the open sea across the rim of her mug. The familiar schooners and sailboats were bobbing up and down on the water, their owners preparing for a day of fishing or sightseeing. An unfamiliar boat was in the harbor that morning too, a small skiff gliding along the white-capped sea, skipping from wave to wave. Its hull was hewn from several dozen strips of thick, rough wood. And its sails had been sewn and patched together with many pieces of fabric, with scraps of sailcloth and at least one bedsheet.

Baxter had built his boat after all, she realized. He'd stayed in Bar Harbor as long as it suited him, and then he'd moved on, trading rocks and pines for sand and palm trees, for the Florida Keys, maybe, or the Caribbean, to see the parts of the world that he and Evie had always hoped to visit.

SUSAN TOLLEFSON
ALLOY PRAYER

Father decants his soul each night
and leaves it in the foundry

where daytime,
men pour molten metal,
forging useful objects.

Sundays he takes me with him.
We plunge through the door,
the cement cold under the soles of our shoes.

We stop before a casting. He reaches through one side of its open core;
I the other

our fingertips touch.

W LUTHER JETT
THE BUSBOY
(Juan Romero, 1951-2018)

Fifty years gone, I still can't sleep.

When I took up that platter
of sandwiches to his room,
the Senator greeted me,
thanked me, shook my hand.

I felt like an American that night.

Came to this country just
a boy, ten years earlier,

(cont)

dust of the Sonora still
hot between my toes.

That was my first job, scarce
out of high school.
I'll never forget how kind
he was, how like a friend.

Bobby.

Twenty-four hours later,
I knelt there, cradling his head
on the cold kitchen floor
while his blood and brains spilled out.

I couldn't wash my hands for days.

First published https://bourgeononline.com/2019/06/two-poems-by-luther-jett/ A historical note: Juan Romero is the hotel worker who came to the aid of Robert (Bobby) Kennedy

Jett

WILLIAM THOMPSON
THE BOOK FINDER

You couldn't always find her. If you went looking for her, you would never find her—that's what some people said. You just had to be in the store—by accident, by chance, or just because.

Most people who claimed to have met her didn't remember her clearly. They would frown, trying to recall.

"I was in there ... a Tuesday, I think," they would say, vaguely. "But I didn't know what I was looking for. Then she came over and just started asking me what I liked to read. I told her ... and she handed me a book."

The stories went like that. Some said it was an older woman—one was convinced it was a man. But most said it was a girl, or a young woman, smiling, inquiring, and asking what you liked to read.

And maybe that was it. You couldn't go into the little shop intentionally. You couldn't walk in and ask for her. If you did, the person behind the counter would say something vague in response: "Oh, you must mean Sarah (or Sally, or Jane). She's not here today, but if you go to the reference desk, someone can help you."

Jo knew someone who had tried—Kat, formerly Katie, who had found Jo on Facebook. They were sitting in Remedy, cautiously catching up—slightly awkward high school acquaintances who were considering becoming friends. Jo sipped her flat-white—a once-a-week indulgence—while Kat drank green tea.

"Have you heard about this woman at the bookstore? You know, the place just down the street."

Jo knew instantly who Kat was talking about, but she didn't let on—not yet. It was too soon for that sort of sharing. They had been talking about books—books each of them had read and books they had in common.

"Who's that?" asked Jo.

"I'm sure it was Fatima who told me first—you remember Fatima? That girl from high school who always carried a book."

"I remember."

"Yeah, well, I ran into her about a month ago. She works for the government, now, you know—something to do with public relations.

"I was getting lunch at one of those food trucks near the Federal building, you know. And there was Fatima. She was carrying a book—just like in high school, always a book in hand.

"Well, I said hi. I told her I've been away from this place for a decade. Now that I'm back I keep running into people from high school. Funny, right?

"Anyway, I must have said something about her still with a book in hand. She gave me this long look—like I'd insulted her or something. I didn't mean to insult her—I was just trying to be friendly, just trying to let her know that I remembered her.

"Then she's telling me about this person in the book store—that if I wanted to find the right book for me, I needed to visit this woman in the book store. It all sounded familiar. So I went to the store. I looked. I even asked at the counter. The guy looked at me like I was nuts."

Jo listened to Kat's story, watching her slightly angular face, with its slightly severe eyebrows, curious green eyes, and firm jawline.

Jo knew two things by the end of the story. She knew that Kat was a quantifier—a measurer of people, of experiences, of lives and intentions. Kat was one of those people who lived her life by reaching out to others, reaching out and performing a demonstrative concern and interest for other people and their lives that was driven by a fundamental core of selfishness, a deep-seated narcissism of which Kat was only partly aware. Jo also knew she and Kat would never be friends.

They parted that afternoon, exchanging numbers and promising to keep in touch. Jo felt mildly violated, as if she had been collected, added to a list or put on a shelf, to later be taken down and displayed for someone else's benefit.

Jo had time before she had to be at the university for her class, so she went to the bookstore—not for any reason, just to look and to spend some time. She wandered up the avenue, watching people walk, singly or in pairs, all bubbled within their own concerns.

Kat wasn't the first person to talk about the woman in the book store, and Jo knew only one or two who had met her. David was the first person she knew who had, but David was blind, so he couldn't say what she looked like. She and David mostly talked by text, but last fall he had called her. He said he had gone into the store one day to find a book on CD. He mostly downloaded his books these days, but he still sometimes liked finding stuff on CD. He didn't know what he was looking for—he had been depressed that week. He'd been having trouble because of his dad's death six months earlier.

"He was a bastard," he said, neutrally. "But you know that—you met him."

A long pause.

"He was a bastard, and now he's dead. I can't change any of that—I can't do anything, now. I only went to see him once in the hospital. I didn't want to go, but I did because of my mom—didn't go back, though. Then he died."

Another pause.

"I haven't been able to put all this together in my head. It's just sort of shitty."

Then he told her about the girl. He said she was just down there in the basement, where they kept the kid's books. David unashamedly loved kid's books. He had taken a course years before, which got him started. And the woman had suggested this book on CD. So he bought it—not that he could afford it. The book hadn't anything to do with his dad, or what he was feeling—not like that. But it helped him get through the next week—then the next, and then things weren't so bad after that.

Jo browsed nonfiction, then fiction. She stopped at corner displays of books, sometimes reaching out to touch the spine of a book or run a finger over a cover—feeling embossed titles and the newness of book jackets.

She paused in an aisle, discovering she was holding a book. She was surprised, looking down and seeing its title. She glanced up, seeing people lined up at the counter. She saw the clock above the counter, stuck at twenty past ten. Outside, it was starting to rain.

Jo ducked into the shelves, only to find a middle-aged woman standing, a little dazedly before a shelf.

"I'm sorry," said Jo, thinking she had almost knocked the woman over.

A small smile. "Don't worry," said the woman. "I'm just standing here. I'm not even sure what I'm looking for."

"I do that all the time," said Jo. "What kind of things do you like?"

"I don't know," said the woman. "All sorts, really. I find lists online and read through them. I read the Governor General winners—things like that. But it's not really enough—if that makes any sense."

"Yes," said Jo, "it does."

And perhaps it was the rain, perhaps it was the feeling of being slightly outside time, outside of anything that was quantifiable, or measurable, or dictated by schedules or the thousand and one things that relentlessly stole one's attention, every day, of every week, of every passing year.

"Here, try this," said Jo, and handed the woman the book, a solid-feeling paperback that wasn't stiff, but pliable and relaxed, the fore-edge untrimmed.

Jo left the woman standing there, engrossed in the book. As she passed the counter, Jo zipped her coat and pulled up her hood. Opening the door, she smelled rain on pavement and a cool hint of decay. On the sidewalk, she paused. For a bewildering second, she saw the street, the traffic, buildings darkened with rain. She looked behind at the entrance to the bookstore. What had she been looking for? She couldn't remember, but she didn't have time to wonder. She had class in half an hour. Jo turned the corner and began the walk up to the university, while the fine October rain pooled on the pavement, hissed beneath the tires of vehicles, and blurred distances into a misty world that seemed to lay forever just out of reach.

ELIZABETH WEIR
INTERMISSION AT LEE BLESSING'S, "GOING TO ST. IVES"
Park Square Theater

"Would you help to kill a brutal dictator?"
a man beside us asks his companion.
We have been watching a woman doctor
wrestle with whether she should aid
in poisoning a ruthless African dictator.
His companion hesitates. "*I'm not sure.*"
"Surely you would have helped to stop Hitler
if you'd known that your decision would prevent
appalling cruelty and save millions of lives?"
She twists her scarf and avoids his gaze.
"You mean to say you don't know how you'd act?"
"*Once you've killed,*" she says, "*it invites a next time,
to back up the purpose of the first. Look at Macbeth
and how one murder led to a long string of killings.*"
"That's fiction. Your ambivalence surprises me."
"*For me to kill another would compromise the core
of who I am. I couldn't continue to live with myself.*"
"Personal well-being becomes irrelevant, here.
We're talking about millions of human lives."
"*In a dictatorship, others, hungry for power,
self-serving as the dictator, will fight to fill the void.
How many others will I find I have to murder?*"
"I thought I knew you. You're not reasoning well."
She sets her chin and faces him. "*Absolute certainty,
underpins the thinking of every dictator.*"
A bell sounds. It's over.

AT SAN FRANCISCO AIRPORT

She wears his red hat, back-to-front,
heavy plait of hair, thick as my wrist,
over her shoulder.

They both chew as they chat.
He plunks his hand, palm side up
on his thigh.

(cont)

She slides her hand over his,
takes it and tucks it tight
under her arm.

He whispers into her ear, and she laughs
out loud, her gum turquoise
on her tongue.

She tugs his ear lobe, hard. He winces,
grinning—such playfulness
between them.

In the dross of crowded airport boredom,
of endless ear-bud conversations
to no one present,

of roller bags and travel-dulled eyes,
these two glint, bright as mica,
in a bed of common shale.

Weir

ELAINE COHEN
YOU CAN'T GO HOME AGAIN

The house I grew up in is derelict. Stripped
of its porch, paint, and pricker-bush hedge,
it sags, lists to starboard, an abandoned
ship in a forgotten port.

 I remember Main Street all lit up at Christmas,
crowded with shoppers, collars turned up
against the cold, the bars in full roar,
stained glass church windows glowing pink,
green, blue, red, yellow, jewel-tones
like the colors running into Cayadutta Creek,
the dyes and mercury and chrome
that poisoned the rivers.

(cont)

Everyone knew Gloversville, NY was doomed.
Growing up, the reason for living was to leave.
One by one, four hundred factories closed.
The people fled. Gone with the gloves.
Main Street today an Edward Hopper still life.
At least it's spring. Trees leafing out,
teenage girls smoking, pushing strollers
on the crooked sidewalks where I once
played hopscotch. Swallows darting forth
from broken factory windows. In the distance
I hear someone practice scales on the piano.
A voice rising in song.

Cohen

TIM MENEES
HOUSE TOUR

    Even in a thin early sun, our foyer catches a shaft of light, as does the Mexican tile on the staircase risers. I imagine Juliana sweeping down the steps and into the living room like Loretta Young did on TV, except no cocktail dress, and neither of us sweeps in anywhere.
    When my wife and I moved south from Seattle, rather Dogfish Island, we looked for a one-level Southwest but settled on a modest two-story with a tile roof. We bought before prices blew out of control, opened it up some and added skylights and windows. Friends have homes that dwarf ours, but how much house do you need?
    The small room on the right I grandiloquently call the library. A Wayne Thiebaud print hangs above a small cabinet. He's famous for painting pastries and candies you could almost eat, but this is of the California Delta, I'm guessing somewhere along the San Joaquin River.
    A clay Mayan fertility goddess sits on a bookshelf between Vladimir Nabokov and James Joyce.
    I've read *Lolita* and *Ulysses,* and they're both funnier than I'd expected.
    We got the small Bronze Age bowl on Cyprus decades ago through embassy friends. It's our one stab at buying fine art.
    I've framed the letters to Dad from FDR (or an aide), to Mom from Frank Sinatra (or his agent), and to Juliana from J.D. Salinger (or his

publisher).

    Across the way is the living room with two small Turkish carpets, a fireplace, and by the sofa a Richard Diebenkorn print. It would be great to have the original paintings, both his and Wayne Thiebaud's, but I don't have hedge-fund-manager loot so I don't collect art (except for that bowl). People glance at them and say, "That's nice," or "Lovely," or worse, "Interesting," but most have never heard of either.

    We shipped the carpets home from Turkey and Morocco. I was stationed in Istanbul during the Cold War. Us versus the Soviets. We knew their guys and vice versa, and neither side had to worry about al-Qaida or ISIS or addled homegrown terrorists. We bought them from Mehmet, a young store owner in the Covered Bazaar, where we also found some copper pots and pans, a Russian samovar, and a glass-and-brass shoeshine box. This was before the Turks caught on and prices, like homes here, shot way up.

    (I was trailed twice. A slim man followed me from the Blue Mosque until I lost him behind Mehmet's place. Maybe he was looking for a bargain to take back to Moscow or Sofia. The second was on a ferry crossing the Bosphorus. He wasn't that good, or maybe he was.)

    The sofa and chair have been in the family from the 1940s.

    I bought the bentwood rocker for Juliana when she was pregnant with our son and put it together myself, hence the gouge on the side where I slipped with the screwdriver.

    The old music box on the gate-leg table plays metal discs and has been in the family since my mother was a tot.

    The aircraft-carrier cribbage board is from Dad after I skunked him one weekend when I was home from college. He learned to play in the Navy during WWII and taught me in the eighth grade. I got pretty good but nobody at Dogfish High up in Washington played, ditto in college. It's a dying game, like pinochle and bridge.

    Overseas we played Hearts.

    The pocket watch is ex-Northern Pacific.

    About the Hammond B3, bunged up, but in college I gigged with a couple bands, and later did a tour with Paul Revere & the Raiders. I considered chasing rock stardom. Talk to any two musicians and most play guitar. Not so with keyboard players. But it's a life of scrambling and penury. Mark Twain said if you become a steamboat captain the river loses all its romance. I'd probably be dead from drugs or alcohol.

    Juliana snagged the "Oh, Lady Be Good," sheet music signed by George Gershwin (supposedly) at a charity auction.

She loves our dining-room table although I'm never sure if it's art deco, arts and crafts, Prairie or Mission. Anyway, who cares? I scrounged up the Tiffany lamp at an antique shop.

The two candlesticks were carved in Alaska. Her great aunt brought them back from Sitka after the war, along with the totem pole in the bathroom. The ancient clock hasn't worked since I was six. The small watercolor could be a Winslow Homer, at least from that era. I keep meaning to get it appraised.

The rose-pattern china is from Juliana's mother, and we use it and the silver. Juliana says why keep them hidden away. Same for the stemware.

We've got some good reds in the wine cabinet, no *grand cru* but better than jug, and most people tell us they're not connoisseurs. We tell them, neither are we.

The "rustic" side board was made by my grandfather.

We did our kitchen in blue and yellow to mimic Giverny. Hence the copper pots and pans. We don't have a lily pond, but we're not artists. The stained-glass window is from an old church on Dogfish Island and we remind friends that for many, cooking is a religion.

I don't know why the old bubble-gum machine is still by the fridge. I set it down there a few years ago and it just sort of stayed. Wayne Thiebaud's painted a couple.

We bought the Fiestaware before it became the darling of the interior-designer crowd.

Upstairs we have three bedrooms and my study. The master has a balcony where Juliana and I drink coffee in the morning. Sometimes we read or I bring out biscotti and pretend we're in Italy. Juliana says I fantasize too much, like I'm unhappy with our life. No. I love it here, and I can't speak Italian.

After the kids left home, we turned their digs into guest rooms, with family photos and prints and furniture we didn't know what to do with. Juliana uses one when she does Christmas cards or announcements for charity events.

In the other, we keep a photo album covered in green velvet that holds photos of forebears who founded Bangor, Maine, and fought in the Civil War, and posed in Union Army jackets, everyone looking unhappier than they probably were. Dad chats with Ike in Germany. Juliana is ten. Packed away is her wedding dress and heels, jewelry, passports from our twenties, my diary from my summer trip hitching through Europe, with names and addresses, a quilt my grandmother made when I was born, a home movie Juliana's dad took during Joe DiMaggio's hitting streak, photos Juliana took of a kid named Elvis performing at some fair. There are letters from me to Mom, from Juliana to her fiancé in Vietnam, and his letters to her before he was killed.

Now my study, an amiable hodgepodge, and in no clear order:
* A vintage pinball machine I keep for its lights and buzzy '50s art.
* A program from a 1965 Rolling Stones concert signed by Mick Jagger. We met through the DJ with the station that promoted the show. It was on a revolving stage, and I wrote a review for the college paper, part of which went:

In those days groups performed their hits plus one new song. Their set list included a cover of Chuck Berry's "Round and Round" and during the sound check Mick told the DJ, "The ladies love it when I grab my balls. Now I can grab them all the way around."

* A model schooner from 1922.
* A Lionel Santa Fe diesel locomotive -- red, yellow and silver, sixty years later, still beautiful. Every Christmas I begged Santa for one, I sang him "Up on the Housetop" and got stiffed. Santa never had enough money. Eventually I turned to eBay.
* Dad's log when he was skipper of a small freighter.
* A popcorn machine with a large glass top, from a long-gone Dogfish Island ferry. We kids could stick our hands inside the spout and jigger a lever for free refills.
* A luger Dad took off a German.
* A prop doorknob from the movie "Psycho."
* A UW football jersey a pal from Dogfish High gave me. He played for the Huskies until he tore up his knee and went into orthodontics.
* A binnacle from a 1930s Puget Sound passenger steamer.
* A letter from a classmate of Mom's who went into the music business and worked with a kid named Richard Penniman, who he said, "gets vulgar but look out." The kid was Little Richard.

#

This morning our neighborhood belongs in a black-and-white newsreel from WWII. Ashes. Smoke. Death. Charred automobiles, part of a wall, a skeleton swing set. A chimney.

That's our house—the chimney.

Twenty miles down the hill the discount-store parking lot has become Tent City. Firefighters catch their breath in the morning haze. We walk around in ill-fitting pants, frayed sweaters, raggedy sneakers and Raiders T-shirts. Tykes run past yelping, why, I can't tell. TV trucks keep vigil along the perimeter while reporters roam through the rubble amid survivors. A Red Cross volunteer hands me a cup of coffee and asks if I need anything. Nothing she can offer.

I could use a drink but I'll wait.

Homeowners insurance. Daughter flying home. It's just stuff. Underwear.

Juliana stands alone, looking up the road, seeing nothing.

MICHAEL MINASSIAN
COMPASSION'S CARRIAGE

A week after Thanksgiving
I see a family huddled
outside the supermarket door—
three generations of women
taking turns holding a sign
with one word: *Hungry*

Shopping carts pass back
and forth, wheels wobbling—
soon it will snow
the sidewalk growing colder—

Inside, the produce already
starting to rot, milk spoil,
the meat and fish turning sour.

(cont)

We think we know
what it is to suffer
but keep our eyes and ears
tuned to what is coming next:
the squeaking wheel,
the bump over the curb
the car's protective shell.

Minassian

HOW TO WRITE A POEM

In the era of turning away,
my students want to know
if it's OK to write about the poor

or the victims of famine
from countries where no one
speaks English or has Wi-Fi—

some compose sonnets
to the war dead and drowned
washing up onto Florida beaches
while downtown Ft. Lauderdale
is on high alert once again—
a priest and rabbi arrested

for feeding the homeless—
the poor and starving
better kept out of sight

let them be hungry—
we have quotas to fill
and poems to write.

Minassian

JOHN GREY
REGARDING MY TIME SPENT IN THE CHOIR

I was a solo tenor
every night
but for Wednesday practice,
all in preparation for Sunday
when I'd be one
of many voices.

My wife understood that
the sounds she heard
emanating from the bedroom
on a Monday or a Friday
were merely a part
of the whole,
should not be judged
by themselves alone.
In other words,
she didn't complain
if I strayed off-key.

She was in the pew on Sunday
listening to the choir,
immersed herself in the massed incantation,
thankfully unable to differentiate
my voice from these others.

No doubt, she loves me for myself
but there are times when
she loves me for how I blend in,
become indistinguishable
from all the others.

It's not up to me
to know which is which.
I defer to my needs.
That's why I can't help singing.

PHIL MERSHON
WHITE CHURCH

I figured mama being white was the only thing that saved her.

The summer of 1965 it didn't rain much. A few low clouds lulled from one end of Nostalgia, Ohio to the other, but I remember the sky didn't drop a speck of rain that weird summer. Mama divided her time between soaking up rays in what I'm sure she thought of as a risqué bikini and the household chores most of the mothers along Pond Creek Road articulated as their holy burdens. In our case, most of those chores involved keeping the house spotless and allergen free. Ever since Dr. Jefferson had performed his famous (i.e. ridiculous) scratch test on my back a year earlier, mama made sure not one speck of dust or dirt felt comfortable in our home. I slept with a dehumidifier running throughout the night, just as I awakened to the sound of mama singing to herself as she rubbed linen dishcloths along the tops of the bookshelves, television, desktops and tables. The bed linens she washed every day. Whenever papa mowed our acreage, mama tucked me into the backseat of our Pontiac Catalina and cranked up the air conditioner to purify the oxygen. All this concern with my respiration instilled me with a paranoia that lingers to this day but which erupted in my youth with voiceless ululations and apoplectic trembles which embarrassed me to no small degree. Like our Dear Lord Jesus, mama would say, I was an only child, which also meant I was all of her children rolled into one—a fate which carried with it a responsibility divided among herself, my father, and Saint Agnes, the patron saint of babysitters.

Mid July of that driest of summers found me two months into my ninth year. From time to time since my birthday at the end of May I had overheard mama and papa expressing concern that their actions on behalf of my supposed allergies might be converting me into something of a weakling, or to quote my father in his own vernacular, "Martha, your goddamned molly-coddling gonna turn that boy into a caramel-colored sissy!" Mama winced whenever papa took the Lord's name in vain and I could picture her face going all pruney even though I listened from behind my bedroom door and couldn't see any of this for myself. What I could also picture in my mind was the sight of papa's hands hanging at his sides. Those hands even when laid upon me in tenderness and affection always scratched my skin like sandpaper. Papa had used those hands on me in punitive ways as well and mama herself had not been immune to the power of those fingered instruments of enforcement. Her reaction, as usual, combined a feigned acceptance with a genuine disapproval.

Another chore mama took upon herself was canning. Mama said that she stored beets, carrots and green beans in Mason jars just in case something tragic should befall us and we would be cut off from the rest of society. It kind of surprised me the way mama took to canning, what with her being a city girl by birth. But papa, having been born and raised less than half a mile from where our house stood—well, he had certain expectations, as he called them, and one of those expectations was that my mama be as much like his own, or at least as much as a big city girl from Columbus could be in a one-time sundown town but now racially integrated podunk village such as Nostalgia.

"William," mama addressed me as I stood before her awaiting instructions. "I want you to fetch me half a dozen Mason jars from that old church down the road. You know the one I mean?"

I knew but wished I didn't.

"If the church is locked, don't worry about it. Just come on back home. It should be open, though. I put a box of jars on a shelf just to the right of that organ or piano in the back. All I need is six or seven for these beets."

I had about as much use for beets as a bulldog has for pajamas. All the same, I understood mama's predicament. She needed to balance out her over-protection of my lungs by sending me into the darkest, dustiest, most Godforsaken vessel of evil it has ever been my misfortune to set foot inside. I sighed, forced a smile, shrugged and trotted out the front door, making my way down the gravel road towards the Birch Township Evangelical Church of Christ.

It was not unusual for people to use the church as a kind of unofficial storage shed, although people tended to give the place a wide girth after dark. Papa always called that house of worship the White Church. He'd told me more than once that, if mama ever instructed me to go to that place, to do as she asked just so long as it was daytime and the sun was out. Otherwise, he'd said, just pretend to go and tell mama the place was locked.

"Now I don't want you making a habit of lying to your mother, boy. For all her highfalutin ways, acting like she knows everything, she's still your mama and you owe her that respect. Between you and me, we also got respect, except it's different. For instance, you know what sanctuary is, boy?"

I had been seven at the time and had no earthly idea.

"Course not. How could you? Sanctuary is what we called it when I was younger than you are now. See, back in my daddy's time, the good old boys would catch strangers passing through after sundown. If them strangers happened to look like you and me, the good boys would nail them to the wooden struts of some old army tent, then set that tent on fire.

Papa pulled his hands out of the pockets of his coveralls. He paced around in a kind of circle, looking at everything except me, pausing to rub his sleeve over his forehead.

"Guys passing through in those days were usually looking for river work. Before you ask, river work was loading, unloading boats ported on the Ohio." He stopped pacing a moment, wiped his head, looked up at the sky and continued pacing. "Honest work it was. Everybody said so.

"Course, honest work meant the kind of work nobody else wanted to dirty their hands on. Let me tell you, William, when any color of man tells you he's got an honest day's work for you, you run in the other direction because what he has for you is either slopping pigs or tickling his privates. You understand?"

I didn't understand but nodded that I did. Papa looked at me, lowered himself so we were eye to eye. He said, "Naw, you don't understand. Not yet. But that day'll come."

Papa stretched back up and resumed his pacing. The sweat lay heavy on him now, as if every word crushed him like a concrete block.

"Well, down the road where your grandpa used to live, some nights you'd hear a hammer hitting nail and the most awful screaming." Papa trembled just a bit, then shook it off. "Worst screaming any of us had heard until a few seconds later when we could smell the sulphur burning. We would hear a band of peckerwood redneck cracker ofays hooting it up while a man they didn't even know burned alive right in front of them."

I could almost feel the chill rolling off papa. He cupped his elbows in his hands to ward off the bite of frost inside him. "That poor man, whoever he might be, he would let out a scream that put a freeze on the night. We'd run outside, your grandpa and me and your grandma, and we'd listen and we would see the night sky roll over like a snake's eyes as it swallows a rat. It was like a message God sent out saying we were on our own.

"The night got real quiet then. The crickets wouldn't natter and the frogs wouldn't croak and even your own heart didn't have the nerve to thump. The blood in your arms and legs just sort of lay still. After a few minutes three or four of them white trash good old boys would come strolling down the road right in front of our house. They'd tip their hats to us all standing together on the porch. One of them would always wish us a good evening. Your grandpa would always nod and wish them the same. Then they and their gunny sacks would disappear into the woods behind my daddy's house. The next morning daddy and me, we'd walk up to the church and we could see the burn patch where what they'd done had been done."

I asked papa why these men had done all this in the churchyard.

Papa didn't pace after that. It was as if my question had brought him back out from whatever overdose of memories had shackled him to the past. Those hands of his released the elbows. He smiled the smile of someone old as Moses and wise as Solomon.

"They done it at the church because they wanted to turn the church bad. See, that old place, back when my daddy was a boy, back when the new free men headed north on their way to Chicago or thereabouts, it was a safe place. A sanctuary. A place where no bullwhips snapped and no ropes got tied and no horses pulled you off in four directions.

"Thing was that the old church was so goddamned sacred that it even scared most of the white men. Some men, William, a very few men full of power and hate, be they white, black, or in between like you, they just don't get scared. A few of these don't-get-scared men set out to make the church a bad place. Nobody'd gone to services there in years so nobody was there to stop them. After a while, the old church that for so many years had been a safe spot for us colored folk, turned into a place where the devil liked to put his feet up and rest."

I replayed this story in my mind on my way there. I passed a big old yellow and black sign that looked as if it had been standing there for years. The sign said "Get us out of the United Nations." I didn't know what that meant other than that around the next corner would be the big old White Church with a rusty chain across the front door.

No padlock would be on the door, but the place was nonetheless guarded. Four wooden steps led from the mouth of the weedy sidewalk up to the door. Beneath those steps swarmed snakes all knotted together like strands of a fisherman's net. Papa always said we only had two types of snakes out our way: good ones and bad ones and the good ones were always dead. The truth was that we had a population of poison snakes—timber rattlers and copperheads—and the safe snakes, like rat snakes, garter snakes, red-bellies and worm snakes. I had no interest getting close enough to tell the venomous variety from the ones that only digested rodents. My interest was to get in and out of the White Church as fast as possible without incident.

As I entered the groping shadow that stretched out onto the gravel road from the Birch Township Evangelical Church of Christ, I saw two white men standing alongside the church on either side of a wheelbarrow, cigarettes hanging off their lower lips and their eyes trained on me. Walking up that sidewalk with the weeds tickling my ankles and the eyes of the two men burning into my skin and the fangs of whatever kind of snakes were untangling themselves underneath the wooden steps, I begged my feet to stop moving even though I was being pulled as if against my strength of will ever closer to that tall white church door.

I recognized the two men. The taller was Robie Shepherd and the other was Smoke Campbell, which he and everyone who knew him pronounced "Camel," like the cigarette. Robie owned a bit of forestry between Pond Creek Road and the Ohio River. Smoke was his hired hand. Neither man was known to favor black folks all that much. One of them said something to me which I didn't catch or care to. I floated up those steps, aware on a subconscious level of a twitchy rattling beneath my feet. My hand tucked itself beneath the length of chain, gripped the ice-cold door handle, and in seconds my shoulder pushed through the barricade of splendor.

Crackles of sunlight through the uneven roof provided the only illumination as there were no windows and only the one set of doors. Webs thick as towing chains draped patterns across the shelves where people had been storing their disposables and unwanted sundries for years. Long dusty beams stretched between the battered ceiling and crusty wooden floor. Fallen crosses leaned against an enormous upright grand piano resting in grandiose solitude at the far end of the church's interior. While I knew nothing about musical instruments, I found myself standing before the Hobart M Cable Cabinet Grand in a state of blind obedience.

The rotting felt on the key hammers smelled like wet wool that had dried and been drenched again. My hands reached out, hovered a moment over the yellowed keys, and played the first few bars of Chopin's "Prelude No 4," a song I had never heard before in my life. No sheet music was provided, nor would it have mattered had it been. The keys pulled my fingertips, moving them across the black and white. I knew the name of the piece, could see the composer working through the repetitious pattern while turning over his shoulder to grin at me just as a rat scurried across the face of one of the fallen crosses and brought me back to a semblance of awareness.

    Those long dusty beams lifted me to what I can only in retrospect consider a weird level of consciousness. Hanging high and overhead swayed a trio of snakes, their eyes rolling over just as papa had described the night sky during the crucifixions. In the same way I found myself knowing Chopin, I knew these snakes to be timber rattlers, or I recognized them as such until they bowed into empty nooses, blowing in no breeze at all.

    The Mason jars to my right trembled on their shelf as if to remind me of my sinister purpose. The sides of the glass containers clinked together like a child's attempt at music until I seized them, brought them to my chest, and continued to feel them vibrate.

    I bolted for the door.

    "What you got there, little boy?" Robie Shepherd asked me as I sailed down the four wooden steps to the weedy sidewalk. "You stealing jars from a church there boy?"

    I didn't slow down. I didn't turn to answer and yet I didn't feel myself making any progress down the walkway. In those moments I knew fear. Being scared made me feel the way I imagined my papa would feel in just that kind of situation. In other words, being scared made me angry.

    "Man asked you a question, boy" said Smoke Campbell. "What you got there?"

    I stopped running. I sat down all but one of the Mason jars. I turned to face the two men. I held out the remaining jar and pointed it at them. I said "What I got is this gun. I will blow your white asses to hell with it."

    What I had between my hands was a Mason jar, clear as day. But I told the two men it was a gun and that must have been what they saw because they pulled their arms out to their sides, they shut up with the stupid questions and they started walking backwards. "We don't want no trouble, boy," Smoke assured me.

    "Then why you still here? Run, you bastards. Run!"

    I fired a round off over their cracker heads and they fell over one another, each clawing and tugging to get ahead of the other.

    Once they were out of sight, I gathered up the other jars and took my time walking back to my house.

    "That didn't take long," mama observed as she liberated the jars from my arms and sat them on the kitchen counter next to a pan of boiling water. "Maybe later you wouldn't mind running a couple of these down to your grandma. She likes beets. Personally, I can't stand the taste and your daddy says he would rather suck flies out of a frog's back side than get near the blessed things."

"I don't like them either," I said, trying to crinkle my nose in disgust.

"It's settled then," mama said as she turned her back. "Why don't you go outside and play? I'll call you in once I get this all put together."

"You want me to go outside and play?"

My mama turned and filled the room with a beautiful smile. "You expected me to send you to your room, I suppose. William? Do you think that I try too hard to save you from the bad things in the world?"

"Too hard?"

"Your daddy thinks maybe I—we—I am making you fragile by protecting you from pollen and ragweed and spinach and all the things Dr. Jefferson said bothered you. What do you think?"

I shifted from one foot to the other. "I like playing outside. I mean, there's no other kids around here. I'm happy in my own company."

"Listen to you. Happy in your own company. You sound just like one of those books you always have your nose buried in. Well, go outside, if that's your liking. But if you get out of breath, you get back inside here fast as you can, okay?"

"Yes, mama."

I ran for the swing set and fell asleep.

The sun had dropped to the horizon when I awakened to the sound of mama screaming. Kids remember their dreams better than do grown-ups, something of a small advantage to being a youngster. The downside is that from time to time children awakening from a dream are less able than their older counterparts to tell the difference between the interrupted dream and the reality into which they have returned. So when mama screamed, I just sort of rolled my head on my shoulders and dismissed the idea that three timber rattler heads were snapping inside jars sitting alone on the kitchen counter.

"What the hell is the matter with you, William?" my papa demanded as he shook me with those big hands of his. I didn't know what time it was, if it was morning or evening, if I was still dreaming or sitting awake in my swing being manhandled by my father, or if Messers Shepherd and Campbell were leading a pack of Night Riders through our backyard, looking for little colored boys to eat, which was how my dream had started out before the movie in my head switched to mama and the snake heads in the jars.

"I asked you what is the matter with you!"

"I—I fell asleep. I—"

Papa let go of my shoulders and used one hand to slap me out of my swing. I hit the ground hard enough to want to cry. But that would just make matters worse, so I pulled myself up and stood beside the swing waiting for the pain to catch up with the smacking.

"I been working all day, William. I ain't even got myself out of the car before I hear your mama cursing a blue streak about snakes and jars and Ba'al Zebul and God knows what else. She's pointing at some goddamned empty jars on the counter, saying snakeheads, snakeheads gonna kill us all. Then she points out the window and there you sit, rocking back 'n' forth in this goddamned swing set of yours like all was right with the world. I picked up one of those jars and shook it at your ma. I told her wasn't nothing in that jar, plain as day. She swoons and I tell her to shut up and then I tore the lid off that jar. Not a goddamned thing in there, William. You know what? I felt something poke at my hand, something like a little tongue and I couldn't see it but I knew it was there."

Papa's face froze so close to my own that I thought he would blot out the sky.

"I slammed that lid back down and your ma went down, too. Fainted dead away. She comes to and all she can say is for me to ask you about them jars. So now I am not asking you, boy. I am demanding you tell me what the bald-headed asshole shit is going on. Don't you lie to me, son. You just speak the truth."

I told papa what I had seen at the White Church. By the time I finished, darkness had pushed the daylight on down the road apiece.

Papa looked me hard in the eyes and told me he was gonna burn that whorehouse church to the ground. "They done turned that place against us, boy. Like when they take a wild stray and hire some Negro to beat at it. 'Fore long that dog hates all black folk. Same thing with that church. Same goddamned thing."

I might have thought papa was crazy, except I knew he wasn't. I may have been just a kid, but that didn't mean I'd forgotten the times when we would be coming home in our Catalina, with mama and papa in the front seats, rolling their windows up without thinking just as we got near the church. You could still feel the heat pouring out of that place, rushing as it did across our car, then gone just as fast once we rounded the bend.

    More than once when lightning would split one of the trees in the back of the churchyard—the sound like an airplane crashing onto the porch—we'd all run out to see that tree axed down the middle and the next day that same tree suffered no damage at all and people would scratch at their heads and walk off mumbling about just how wrong a person could be.

    Every now and again somebody would disappear after getting too close to that church, like the time Smoke Campbell's teenage girl, Becky, went missing after she had banged on our front door, asking mama if she could please use our bathroom and mama saying she figured Mr. Campbell wouldn't approve of that. Becky—I was maybe six or seven when she disappeared—she told my mama that she would just lift her skirt out behind the old church if that was the way we felt about it. No one saw Becky again after that, until somebody—I think it was Robie Shepherd, but I'm not sure—suggested the police check out the chimney at the old church on account of you know how kids are, they're just curious like animals sneaking around places where they shouldn't. Sure enough her charred body was stuck halfway up that fireplace chimney, and when the police finally got her body to fall, they said that both her arms had been gnawed off at the shoulders.

    Nobody ever got around to asking Robie or whoever it had been how come he'd thought to suggest Becky was stuck in the chimney, what with that being among the luckier guesses wandering around. I suppose the authorities might have been too sick and put off by the condition that girl was in to think about asking any kind of useful questions. That or they figured one teenage white trash city goat wasn't worth any more bother than she'd been already.

    While I'd been woolgathering, papa had been raving as if all of mama's subtleties had at last gotten through to him. The abolition of sin, the purification of fire, crossroads where blues hounds came in ignorant and came out hypnotized—papa's face glowed stronger with the mention of each of these. As for myself, I could think of no reason to argue about any of it. I felt the flames of justice welling inside me. I felt the shatter as the church collapsed. I knew the roar of Satan's frustration at the destruction of his palace.

    Papa's big hands opened our back door. He and I walked inside together. We saw mama pressed back against a far wall, refusing to take her eyes off those empty Mason jars. Papa scooped them up and jammed them into his oversized pockets.

    Time speeded and slowed like a racehorse somebody drugged. While papa gathered things we would need for the proper burning, I sat mama down and explained what we intended to do. Had this been a normal time, mama would have locked me in my bedroom with the dehumidifier on full blast. Instead, she stared into my eyes, looking for something there that would at least let her know what questions to ask. I was about to say something when I felt papa's hand fall on my shoulder. He said, "Martha, I think you should come with me and the boy."

    I was careful not to shine the light on the four steps leading up to the church door based on the idea that the only thing worse than a snake bite would be seeing the snake look at you before it sunk its fangs in deep. The three of us—mama having surprised me and papa by insisting she go along—placed each of our five-gallon cans of kerosene in three corners of the church.

    After those were in place, I trained the light on that ceiling beam. Those snakes or ropes or whatever they were still hung there swinging in the nonexistent breeze.

    The church being surrounded by dried trees and a drier forest behind it, papa went outside to lay up some metal poles against all the sides of the church to keep the fire from spreading and maybe burning down most of Pond Creek Road.

    Daddy popped his head back in to tell us to wait inside and when he came back he was toting an axe which he used to bash away at the chimney. He told us the smoke needed to be able to escape or else the "goddamned place" might blow off the roof and settle down on somebody's house and the fire would wipe them out. After he threw the axe at the base of the fireplace he motioned mama and me to get ready. Papa pulled those three Mason jars out of his front pockets and tossed them gently onto the keys. He pulled a can of lighter fluid out the back pocket, spraying it on that piano, right next to where the jars had landed. All kinds of little things scattered out of that device as if they knew what was about to happen. I thought mama might pass out but instead she just held onto me. We watched as papa threw the empty can across the room and lit a stick match on the sole of his shoe.

    Orange and black and blue flames shot up from inside the old piano. A scream like one hundred cows at slaughter roared out of that thing. I dropped the flashlight by accident. It didn't matter because I could see mama from the blaze and I could see papa backing away from it, signaling mama and me to get on out of there. We stepped back and back and back, yet didn't seem to make progress getting closer to the front door. Long strands of webbing fell from above us as the flames took hold of the walls on their way to those cans of kerosene.

Papa turned to us and told us to run, goddammit, and just as we were turning towards the front door, a bolt of fire leapt out of the center of that old piano, arched itself up high, then shot like it might be a beam of fire lightning right through papa's back and out the front of his chest.

The last thing mama and I saw was papa's eyes sort of pleading with us to go on, get away, get out of that evil place.

By the time we reached Pond Creek Road, the howling from the church bored into our ears like electric wires. The cans of kerosene breached in the way of a levy holding back fire. Without turning to look, I could feel the walls of the church splintering apart, inhaling the night air, gathering up whatever dormant demons had found refuge there. Mama tried to say something to me, but I couldn't make out a word. I grabbed her hand and we both stopped running. She pulled me to her and said with total clarity, "God must be drunk tonight." We turned around and the White Church glowed in what I can only describe as an arrogant majesty, proud as it was of its own behavior.

We didn't sleep at all that night, as you might expect. Mama and I just sat together on the kitchen floor, staring at our front door as if somehow papa would come walking through with an angry grin, wanting to know when the hell we were going to eat dinner.

Papa wasn't coming back.

Mama fell asleep a little after sunrise. I slipped out from under her arms and made careful not to wake her as I crept out our front door and on down our driveway with the Catalina parked in it. I walked in no particular hurry out onto Pond Creek Road and in a few minutes I passed the sign about getting out of the United Nations, except the sign said "Don't let the sun catch you going down" before it changed back to its original message.

A few feet later I could see the eastern sun cast shadow of the White Church and I knew before I got there—I knew from the shadow the church would stand there unharmed.

No smoke, no soot, no sounds of cattle roaring. Nothing was there except the Birch Township Evangelical Church of Christ, "Prelude No 4" tapping itself out from behind those white walls, plus Smoke Campbell and Robie Shepherd standing outside just as they had the day before.

"What you doing back here, boy?" Shepherd said. "You ain't looking for nobody, is you?"

Campbell said, "See you ain't got no gun today, boy. That right?"

Smoke Campbell laughed and his laughter joined with that of Robie Shepherd as I turned and ran back to mama who was still asleep on the floor. I crawled back beneath the safety of her white arms.

PAULA YUP
MILK BOTTLE

full of people
where order a Reuban sandwich
a side of salad
with ranch dressing

celebrate my 34th anniversary
tomorrow May 4, 2019
but never happen

husband passed
soon after Christmas
sepsis failing kidney
made a liver transplant
impossible

but he passed happy
expecting to wake up in Seattle
with a new liver

last words he said to me
when visiting hours ended at six
"Bye sweetie."
Five years ago

(cont)

we celebrated my 57th birthday
eating Reuban sandwiches
my husband's favorite
so I celebrate again
all alone

Yup

CINCO DE MAYO

without my husband
our 34th anniversary May 4th
over
felt lost without
my love
saw a friend
watched *Star Wars* on TV
remember Quaker meeting
on Cape Cod
the first time I saw *Star Wars*
my husband couldn't believe
I'd never seen it before
and now I can't believe
my husband not around
to eat dinner at Rancho Chico
to celebrate
like we did for our 33rd
anniversary
if only he'd gotten a liver
before his body failed
in his 61st year
my rage a fire I can't quench

Yup

TAMRA WILSON
STEVE'S ASHES

When Aunt Shirley called to say that Steve had died and would I please help with the ashes, I had no idea what I was in for. I wasn't surprised that Steve had passed. He'd lingered a good while with lung cancer.

"You will help lay him to rest?" she said.

Steve and I had grown up together. I thought of him more as a brother than a second cousin.

The Colletons aren't flush with worldly goods and funeral expenses aren't what they care to spend on. Live hard, party hard. That's the way Steve would have wanted it, along with a cold long-necked bottle of Budweiser. Thanks to cancer, he got his wishes.

The family looked over the options and chose cremation, the cheapest. No expensive suit, flowers, hearse.

"Steve liked the idea of being scattered," Shirley said. "We're taking him over to your daddy's fish pond," Shirley said, her voice cracking. "He liked fishing there, you know."

I knew. We'd practically grown up on the south end of a fishing pole. Largemouth, sunfish, brim, catfish, you name it, we caught it until the Mexicans moved in to work the carpet mill, we pretty much had the place to ourselves. We'd swim the pond, careful not to get snagged in tangled lines. Steve loved to tread out to the deepest part of the pond where the big cats bred, and sink himself under the boat. When I thought he'd drowned, he'd surface on the other side. Steve's daddy had run the foreigners off until his rheumatism kept him from walking all the way out there. Before long we were outnumbered and he gave up. And at last, so had Steve.

Somehow he had picked me to be his sole pall bearer. "Buddy will take you out and we'll have him in a box," Shirley said.

"Sure," I said, wondering how I'd get off work. They don't take too kindly to folks taking off from Wal-Mart, especially on a Saturday, which was when the service was to be, if you could call it that.

I showed up in my Sunday pants and dress shirt, no tie. Steve never wore one and he sure wasn't wearing one now, all packed into a space the size of a tackle box. The container was nice enough, a male floral pattern if you could call it that. I figured Aunt Shirley had picked it out, made of some kind of cardboard. I reckon it weighed at least seven pounds. Steve was a heavy-set man; I had no idea he would boil down to something so small.

The Colletons lined one side of the pond all in their best jeans and t-shirts. Most wore sunglasses since it was close to three o'clock. Each of them carried a long-necked Budweiser, a special brew for the occasion.

There hadn't been a funeral, though the Martins would have liked for there to be one. The Martins were Steve's Mama's relatives, all Methodists from over around Whiteville. I haven't got anything against town Methodists. They commenced to singing "Shall We Gather at the River" though this was a spring-fed pond. They sweated gently in their khakis and sports shirts—"city-rich," Steve called them. The Colletons, not to want to press their luck with drinking songs, held quiet.

Aunt Shirley read a poem, something from Billy Graham's newspaper column, and then she raised her right hand to give Buddy the cue. We trolled out toward the middle of the pond where it's good and deep. Steve and I had done our share of belly flops off his daddy's john boat, this very same craft we were riding in. I wanted to cry, but I held up. Steve would have wanted me to be strong.

I lifted the box and Buddy helped me lower is gently into the water as if, on cue, the Colletons raised their long-neck Buds in unison. Then Buddy snapped the cap off his beer and poured it onto the box as Steve had asked.

I'd never seen anything work out so perfectly. Steve, who'd had plenty of time to think about his exit, had this planned out straighter than a jig line. A few bubbles rose to the surface. As Buddy cranked the trolling motor, I noticed that the box had somehow made its way to the backside of the boat. "He ain't goin' down easy," I said.

"We can't let him stay there," Buddy said. I could hear what he was thinking Some kids would find the box, think it was pretty and lug it home. There'd be Steve on display on some house trailer, or later, fertilizer for okra and tomatoes, not that Steve wouldn't make good on such a task.

"We can't let him float," Buddy urged. He rolled his eyes back to the shoreline. The Colletons and the Martins were watching, "They'll take him for a bait box."

I was sure he was right. Then Buddy reached into the water—the side that couldn't be seen from that crowd on the shore—and gentled the floating box to the side of the boat with his index finger and motioned for me to slit the top wide enough to dump the ashes into the water, like scattering crumbs on the surface. The white specs, all that was left of

Steve, swirled like a miniature galaxy.

    The Martins were still singing as we worked, oblivious to what we were contending with in the middle of the fish pond.

    "They ain't none the wiser," Buddy said. "Steve ain't gonna wind up in no trailer park."

    No indeed. I took another sip of my Bud and pondered the universality of it all. How Steve, a big hunk of a man, had been reduced to almost nothing; not what he'd hoped for but what he got: stardust that won't sink.

ALISON STONE
FRIENDS ARE STARTING TO DO STUFF TO THEIR FACES

I'm not sure what's more disconcerting –
the pumpkin cheeks or arched, immobile brows
of a botched job, or, when it works,
women in their fifties suddenly smooth-skinned,
looking like they have no kids and spent
the last decade resting poolside
sipping kale juice with a reflexologist on call.
Even a pal who vows she'll never,
one day pulls her face up, sighs,
I know I'd look much better,
but it's so expensive.
My objection's principle – not
that I'm serene about the furrows and blotches,
but I hope to be, and how can any of us
find beauty in normal aging
if we never see it? My puppy,
joyfully licking my face when I say *walk*,
knows what's important. Nose-led,
she frolics until I jerk her back
from our neighbor's yard, a yellow
pesticide warning sign bright against
the glossy, artificial-looking green.
My property's no eyesore. I have the same
forsythia and daffodils. Just as many tulips.

(cont)

Bleeding hearts to boot.
True, the grass is mottled, but that's
nothing soft lighting wouldn't fix,
or a bright tree to distract the eye
from the fetch path the dog
wore from fence line to stairs.
Let's surrender to my lawn's uneven tones,
accept that thorned vines
wrap themselves around the rhododendron.
And the dandelions are advancing.

MARGARET HERMES
THE OFF-SEASON

So I'm a bitch not to feel grateful.

Jen and Kevin have turned cartwheels to cheer me. They've smothered me in down, tempted me with ambrosia stolen from the lips of the loathsome gods. And what is there to say about The Cabin except that it's palatial on a terribly tasteful, minimalist scale?

They've given me all of Lake Michigan, so when I cannot bear the claustrophobia of their generosity another millisecond, I steal down to the beach, settle gingerly onto one of the three white Adirondack chairs amid the spears of dune grass. Their hospitality can be measured by their never following me here. The other chairs sit empty while I stare out uninterrupted, seeing everything in all directions, like a fly.

Though still the off-season, the days have lengthened during the weeks I've ruled over all I see. The weekenders are not yet whirring about, frantic June bugs cramming into two days as much as necessary to justify their Michiana mortgages. There's hardly anyone around to notice me. Knees drawn up to chin, I sit hugging myself like an orphan. It's still chilly here and lately I'm cold all the time, no matter the temperature, but I'm bundled more against the world than the weather. Baseball cap pulled down, jacket collar turned up—you'd need to come very close to discover I have no eyebrows.

When Terry disappeared three weeks to the day after my surgery, I faced two grieving processes simultaneously. Eleven grinding, bumper-to-bumper months later, I know it's better that he's gone. I don't have to take care of him, nurse him through my illness, spare him my pain.

Saints Jen and Kevin don't require me to appreciate the crap they do to brighten my dark days. They also don't call me on the crap I dish out. Must really suck to be them.

This morning I puked before breakfast. And before I made it to the bathroom. Kevin must have heard me retching. He barged into the bedroom without apology, helped me back to bed. After tossing me a clean towel, he shoved the wastebasket in the vicinity of the pillow and went after my bile with a roll of paper towels. "The saddest thing about losing Mr. McGregor," Kevin said, speaking of their yellow Lab flattened by a Volvo two years ago, "was that you could always count on him to clean up the vomit." I remember Mr. McGregor. Kevin lies.

Three hours later, Jen came into the bedroom holding a Sucrets lozenge tin like it was a wounded bird. Inside the tin casket lay three neatly mummified joints.

"Where would *you* get these?"

Jen and Kevin have always served on the frontlines in the War On Drugs.

"The kid who runs the bike shop," Jen said. "He has a crush on me."

"I hope they didn't cost you too much," I said. But, for a moment, I hoped they did. Cost her. A copped feel in the backroom of the bike shop. A sordid afternoon at a dingy motel. Her perfect marriage. "Sorry," I said, though she'll never know what I was apologizing for.

"I just hope this helps," she said.

"It will."

And it did. That bestowal almost makes up for the Easy Bake Oven my parents never bought me, the free ride to grad school that I missed, the white wedding, the key to the locked door of happiness.

I'm out here on my chair and into my field of bug vision comes this guy and his big, wet dog. The guy is young, though probably not any younger than the kid with connections who has a crush on Jen. The dog's young too. If we could harness the energy in that tail, we could power a dozen mammography machines.

The dog is pawing at something floating at the edge of the shore. It drags a piece of driftwood at least five feet long and as thick as a man's arm. The dog presents the limb, but its owner continues on, bent ninety degrees, reading the lake rocks as if they are his biography.

The dog tries to snatch the limb again but the tide has teased it out. After nosing the driftwood back to shore, the dog latches on near an end but is unbalanced by the length, releases it and scouts for the middle, clamping it, this time successfully. Head high, it parades behind its master like a show dog. I sit up. The limb is so much longer than the dog and so fat my jaws ache, but the dog prances on until its owner stoops to excavate a rock protruding from the sand.

The dog trots in front of its master and drops its prize. The master pretends he doesn't see the wood. He pretends he has eyes only for quartz and granite. At last he picks up the driftwood and plays at balancing it upright on his palm. Finally, he swings it far back with both arms, like a colossal baseball bat, and lets it sail out into the lake. The dog charges into the water, capturing the limb at its precise middle, and returns. Again, his keeper feigns rockblindness before condescending to send the skeleton branch out upon the waves. I watch this scene and its variations a dozen times until dog and master sink out of sight behind a dune.

What kind of dog would put itself through this ordeal, I ask myself. Again and again. And then some more. A Dumb Dog is the answer I expect to dredge up but, instead, A Retriever pops into my head like a gift. A *golden* retriever living wholly in the moment. A glorious moment of struggle that leaves a dog panting for more.

Tomorrow I won't think of glory when I think struggle, but I might recollect the retriever. That and the remaining joints and the unstinting martyrdom of friends could see me through another day.

CONTRIBUTORS

LINDSEY ANDERSON is an Ohio-born, Wisconsin-based journalist covering art and culture in her adopted state. In her free time she can often be found wandering through museums or curled up on her couch with her dog, a local brew and a good book.

ELIZABETH STANDING BEAR dreams big: wants to see her 1806-1930 epic on the big screen. Her character, Holly Patterson, came from a small dream about sitting on the porch swing in the dark, hearing the rain on the roof, watching as lightening lit up the lane and the barn across the road, when a car paused at the end of the lane and put something out. And the story began.

STEVEN BEAUCHAMP is a Professor Emeritus of English for Georgia Perimeter College, a multi-campus two-year college in the metro Atlanta area. He spends most of the year in Florida. For some years he edited poetry for the literary magazine, the *Chattahoochee Review*. During the past 25 years he has published 95 poems in journals and reviews across the US and in Canada. These include the *Kansas Quarterly, the South Carolina Review, The Ecclectic Muse,* and many others.

STEPHEN BOULHOSA was born, raised and currently resides with his wife and three daughters in the hills of Yonkers, NY. Always one to take full advantage of his hometown's proximity to New York City, he has read in several and even won some poetry slams at the famed Nuyorican Poets Cafe. He is a graduate of Fordham University and works in the healthcare industry. His poetry has appeared in *Alternative Motifs.*

PETER BREYER has worked as a health care consultant while pursuing his passion for building and writing. He currently spends his time in the Berkshire Hills of New York growing CBD hemp. His books are available on Amazon and his short stories, under his pseudonym Max Bayer, appear in numerous journals.

ELAINE COHEN is author of three poetry chapbooks and has recently completed a full-length volume of poems. She coauthored *Unfinished Dream: The Musical World of Red Callender,* (Quartet Books, London) and wrote about jazz and new music in California and New York City. Originally from upstate New York, she has lived on Cape Cod since 2003.

MICHAEL COHEN is the author of *Rivertown Heroes* and *The Three of Us*. His short stories have appeared in *Streetlight, Adelaide, STORGY, Umbrella Factory, FRiGG Magazines,* and *The American Writers* and *Penman Reviews*. His stories will appear/have appeared in *The North Dakota Quarterly, Evening Street Review, and Litbreak Magazine.* A retired lawyer, he lives with his family in Seattle. mikecohenauthor.com; Facebook: Michael Cohen Author.

J F CONNOLLY retired after forty-seven years of teaching and has published more than 100 poems and several short stories. His latest work is *Picking Up The Bodies.*

PAUL C DALMAS is a freelance writer who has made his living as boilermaker's helper, a fry cook, and a high school English teacher. His work has been broadcast on KQED-FM and published in *Newsweek, The San Francisco Chronicle* and *California Magazine.* He lives in Berkeley, CA.

MARTHA K DAVIS is the author of the novel *Scissors, Paper, Stone* (2018), which won the Quill Prose Award. She earned an MFA in Fiction from Columbia University. Her short stories and essays have appeared in *River Styx, StoryQuarterly, The Gay & Lesbian Review, Stone Canoe,* and other literary magazines as well as several anthologies.

HOLLY DAY's newest poetry collections are *In This Place, She Is Her Own* (Vegetarian Alcoholic Press), *A Wall to Protect Your Eyes* (Pski's Porch Publishing), *I'm in a Place Where Reason Went Missing* (Main Street Rag Publishing Co.), *Folios of Dried Flowers and Pressed Birds* (Cyberwit.net), *Where We Went Wrong* (Clare Songbirds Publishing), *Into the Cracks* (Golden Antelope), and *Cross-Referencing a Book of Summer* (Silver Bow Publishing).

JAMES DOYLE was born in upstate New York and when his father gained sole custody of him when he was 12, they moved to Florida. After ten years of poor decisions and addiction, he took a human life. But out of a life sentence emerged new life. "Writing became my means of self-expression and growth. Now, it is a blessing to share my experience with others."

DEBORAH FLEMING's most recent book is *Resurrection of the Wild: Meditations on Ohio's Natural Landscape.* She has published two collections of poems, two chapbooks, one novel, and four volumes of scholarship. Winner of a Vandewater Poetry Award and grants from the National Endowment for the Humanities and National Council of Learned Societies, she has had three poems nominated for the Pushcart Prize. Currently she is editor and director of the Ashland Poetry Press.

JAMES FOWLER teaches literature at the University of Central Arkansas. His poems have recently appeared in such journals as *Futures Trading Magazine, Sheila-Na-Gig, Cave Region Review, Elder Mountain, Cantos, Valley Voices, Aji Magazine, Westview, Malevolent Soap, Seems, Angry Old Man Magazine, Dash,* and *Common Ground Review.* He has pieces forthcoming in *Gyroscope Review, Lullwater Review,* and *The Poetry of Capital.*

BRAD G GARBER has degrees in biology, chemistry and law. He writes, paints, draws, photographs, hunts for mushrooms and snakes, and runs around naked in the Great Northwest. Since 1991, he has published poetry, essays and weird stuff in such publications as *Edge Literary Journal, Pure Slush, Burningword Literary Journal, Third Wednesday, Barrow Street, Barzakh Magazine, Ginosko Journal, Slab, Panoplyzine, Split Rock Review, Smoky Blue Literary Magazine, The Offbeat* and other quality publications. He was a 2013 and 2018 Pushcart Prize nominee.

ARTHUR GINSBERG, a neurologist and poet based in Seattle, has studied poetry with Galway Kinnell, Sharon Olds, and Lucille Clifton. His work appears in the anthologies, *Blood and Bone* and *Primary Care,* from University of Iowa Press. He won the William Stafford prize in 2003. His MFA degree in creative writing in 2010 is from Pacific University where he studied with Dorianne Laux, Marvin Bell and David St. John. His book, *The Anatomist,* was published in 2013. He teaches "Brain and the Healing Power of Poetry" at the University of Washington.

ROBERT GRANADER has published more than 350 articles and essays in over fifty publications. After a stint as a journalist covering Capitol Hill in Washington, DC, he has been the CEO of MarketResearch.com for 20 years. His writing focuses on the struggle of the middle-aged man and coping with his changing world as he is no longer in the middle of anything. More at RobGranader.com or expatlondon.blogspot.com.

JOHN GREY is an Australian poet, US resident. Recently published in *Midwest Quarterly, Poetry East* and *North Dakota Quarterly* with work upcoming in *South Florida Poetry Journal, Hawaii Review* and *Roanoke Review*.

MEREDITH DAVIES HADAWAY is the author of three poetry collections: *Fishing Secrets of the Dead, The River is a Reason*, and *At The Narrows* (winner of the 2015 Delmarva Book Prize for Creative Writing). She holds an MFA in Poetry from Vermont College of Fine Arts. She is a former Rose O'Neill Writer-in-Residence at Washington College where she taught ecopoetry and served as chief marketing officer.

MARGARET HERMES has a novel coming out in fall of 2020 with Delphinium Books. Her story collection *Relative Strangers* (Carolina Wren/Blair) was chosen by Jill McCorkle for the Doris Bakwin Book Award. Dozens of other stories have appeared in journals such as *The Missouri Review* and *The Literary Review*. Her published/performed work includes a mystery novel, *The Phoenix Nest*, and a stage adaptation of an Oscar Wilde fable. When not writing, she concentrates on environmental issues.

DAVID JAMES has two new books coming out in 2020: *A Gem of Truth* and *Nail Yourself into Bliss*. More than thirty of his one-act plays have been produced; he teaches writing at Oakland Community College in Michigan.

W LUTHER JETT is a native of Montgomery County, Maryland and a retired special educator. His poetry has been published in numerous journals as well as several anthologies. He is the author of two poetry chapbooks: *Not Quite: Poems Written in Search of My Father* (Finishing Line Press, 2015) and *Our Situation* (Prolific Press, 2018).

HAVA KOHL–RIGGS lives on a Greek island with her dog, Molly. Previously, she lived in Israel, and before that, Madison, WI, where she was married, raised two sons, worked as the cantorial soloist for her synagogue, and had a career as a psychotherapist. She continues to work as a life coach by telephone from her refuge in Greece where she paints, writes, hikes, swims and knits for her two delightful grandchildren.

JOHN KRUMBERGER has previously published a volume of poems entitled *The Language of Rain and Wind* (Backwaters Press, 2008) and a chapbook, *In a Jar Somewhere* (Black Dirt Press, 1999). His latest collection is *Because Autumn*

(Main Street Rag Press, 2016). He works as a psychologist in private practice in St. Paul, MN and lives with his wife in Minneapolis.

IAIN MACDONALD, born and raised in Glasgow, Scotland, currently lives in Arcata, California. He has earned his bread and beer in various ways, from flower picker to factory hand, merchant marine officer to high school teacher. His first two chapbooks, *Plotting the Course* and *Transit Report*, were published by March Street Press, while a third, *The Wrecker's Yard*, was released by Kattywompus Press.

TESSA SMITH MCGOVERN is a British writer living in the US and currently pursuing an MFA in Writing at the Vermont College of Fine Arts. She's the author of *London Road: Linked Stories* (eChook Digital Publishing), *Cocktails for Book Lovers* (Sourcebooks, Inc) and many short stories. Her novel in progress, *The Selkie Daughter*, is a modern retelling of the selkie myth. Learn more at tessasmithmcgovern.com.

TIM MENEES grew up in Seattle. He later drew editorial cartoons at the morning paper in Pittsburgh for 30 years. His work appeared in national newspapers and news magazines. The online journals *Ariel Chart, Smoky Blue Literary and Arts Magazine, Pilcrow & Dagger* and *The Broadkill Review* have published his short stories. His nonfiction pieces appear in *Boomer Cafe*. Today he cartoons and writes for *The Pittsburgh Quarterly*, paints and plays the piano.

PHIL MERSHON has been dipping his quill since 2000, writing for technical journals, music magazines, literary publications, and humor editions for various radio programs. He recently moved from Arizona to West Virginia and expects the transition to take several decades.

MICHAEL MINASSIAN is a contributing editor for *Verse-Virtual*, an online magazine. His chapbooks include poetry: *The Arboriculturist* (2010); *Chuncheon Journal* (2019); and photography: *Around the Bend* (2017). For more information: michaelminassian.com

ALEXANDER PAYNE MORGAN has been published in *The MacGuffin, Crack The Spine, Peninsula Poets, Sequestrum*, and *Dunes Review*, among others. He won the 2016 Kay Murphy Prize for Poetry by *Bayou Magazine* as well as first prize for poetry in the Springfed Arts writing contest in 2015. His chapbooks *Loneliness Among Primates*, 2018, and *H.G. Wells Investigates the Tragedy of Colour in America*, 2019, were published by Kelsay Books.

AARON PARKER is a member of the Evening Street Press DIY Prison Project eveningstreetpress.com/diy-prison-project.html

STEVEN PELCMAN has been published in *The Windsor Review, The Innisfree Poetry Journal, The Fourth River* magazine, *River Oak Review, Poetry Salzburg*

Review, *The Baltimore Review*, *The Warwick Review*, *The Greensboro Review*, etc. He was nominated for the 2012 Pushcart Prize for individual poems and his volume of poetry, *like water to STONE* (Adelaide Books), was nominated for the 2017 Pushcart prize. His other books are: *American Voices*, Outlaws Publishing 2017 and *Where the Leaves Darken*, 2018 Adelaide Books. Poetry Reading: Steven Pelcman @ the University of Education Karlsruhe

EDWARD RIELLY is a professor emeritus at Saint Joseph's College in Maine, where he created and directed the college's Writing and Publishing program. His most recent books are *Beautiful Lightning: Spiritual Poems in a Difficult World*; the memoir *Bread Pudding and Other Memories: A Boyhood on the Farm*; *Answers Instead: A Life in Haiku*, and the children's picture books *Spring Rain Winter Snow* and *Jugo Meets a Poet*.

ZACK ROGOW is the author, editor, or translator of more than twenty books and plays. His poetry collections include *Irreverent Litanies*, *The Number Before Infinity*, and *Talking with the Radio*. His coauthored play *Colette Uncensored* had a reading at the Kennedy Center in Washington DC, and ran in London, San Francisco, and Portland. His blog, *Advice for Writers*, has more than 200 posts. He serves as a contributing editor of *Catamaran Literary Reader*. www.zackrogow.com

PATRICK SHATTUCK has been teaching English in high school and junior college for the past twenty-five years. Additionally, he is also a dedicated writer—he received his B.A. in English from Syracuse University and his M.A. in English from Simmons College in Boston. His short stories and poetry have been published in the *Antietam Review*, *Smashing Icons*, *Lonesome Traveler*, *Paradigm Magazine*, *Fox Cry Magazine*, and *The Syracuse University Review*. He currently lives in California.

JAN SHOEMAKER is the author of the essay collection, *Flesh and Stones: Field Notes from a Finite World*, and the poetry collection, *The Reliquary Earth*. Her work has been anthologized, featured on public radio, and published in many magazines and journals. She lives in Michigan.

ALISON STONE has published six full-length collections, *Caught in the Myth* (NYQ Books, 2019), *Dazzle* (Jacar Press, 2017), *Masterplan*, collaborative poems with Eric Greinke (Presa Press, 2018), *Ordinary Magic*, (NYQ Books, 2016), *Dangerous Enough* (Presa Press 2014), and *They Sing at Midnight*, which won the 2003 Many Mountains Moving Poetry Award; as well as three chapbooks. She has been awarded *Poetry*'s Frederick Bock Prize and *New York Quarterly*'s Madeline Sadin Award. www.stonepoetry.org www.stonetarot.com

WILLIAM THOMPSON is totally blind. He teaches children's literature for MacEwan University in Edmonton, Canada. His fiction and nonfiction has appeared in *Penmen Review*, *Literary Orphans*, *Hippocampus Magazine*, and

Wanderlust. He has two collections of stories, *The Paper Man and Other Stories*, and *Fractured and Other Fairy Tales*, both available on Amazon. He also maintains a blog at www.OfOtherWorlds.ca, and he loves to walk and read, usually at the same time.

SUSAN TOLLEFSON has a BA in mass communications from Purdue University and an MFA in creative writing from Vermont College. Now retired, she has worked as a reporter, photographer, writer, editor, and publications director. Her poetry placed as runner-up in the Wisconsin Academy Review Poetry Contest, 2006, and she has studied with Gordon Mennenga and Laurel Yourke. Besides writing, she loves visual art; she is an urban sketcher and a landscape painter.

RACHEL TRAMONTE lives with her partner and their two daughters in Cleveland, OH. Her work has appeared in *Jelly Bucket*, *Slab*, *Green Hills Literary Lantern*, *The Alembic*, *Third Wednesday*, and other journals.

JEAN VARDA's poetry has appeared in: *The Berkeley Poetry Review*, *Poetry Motel*, *Manzanita Poetry & Prose of the Mother Lode & Sierra*, *Avocet A Journal of Nature Poems*, *California Quarterly*, *Third Wednesday* and *The Red River Review*. She has been nominated twice for a Pushcart Prize. She has taught poetry writing workshops, hosted a poetry radio show and sponsored poetry events at cafes. She also is a collage artist, her way to escape words. She lives in Chico, CA, where she works as a nurse and artist.

WILL WALKER lives in San Francisco with his wife and their dog. He's a former editor of the *Haight Ashbury Literary Journal*. He has studied with many poets over the years, including Marie Howe, Robert Pinsky, and Alan Shapiro. But his main claim to fame is having pizza with J. D. Salinger in Claremont, NH.

ELIZABETH WEIR lives in Minnesota. Her book of poetry, *High on Table Mountain*, was published by North Star Press in March 2016 and was nominated for the 2016 Midwest Book Award. Publications include *Evening Street Review*, *Comstock Review*, *Talking Stick*, *The Kerf*, *Water ~ Stone Review*, and Holy Cow! Press anthologies. She has received four SASE/Jerome Awards.

GLEN WEISSENBERGER, a Harvard Law School graduate, has distinguished himself as a trial lawyer, a law professor, a legal scholar and a law school dean. After four decades in the legal profession, he began a second career devoted to writing short stories and novels. His stories have appeared in *SLAB*, *The Broadkill Review* and *Boston University Law Review*. His legal books and articles are consulted and cited extensively by judges and lawyers.

TAMRA WILSON lives within sight of the Blue Ridge Mountains and is a Road Scholar speaker for the NC Humanities Council, specializing in Southern literature and American history. Stories in her collection, *Dining with Robert*

Redford, have appeared in *Epiphany, North Carolina Literary Review, The MacGuffin* and elsewhere. She is also co-editor of *Idol Talk: Women Writers on the Teenage Infatuations That Changed Their Lives*, 2018 (McFarland).

HIROMI YOSHIDA Hiromi Yoshida is recognized as one of Bloomington's "finest and most outspoken poets," and a semi-finalist for the 2018 Wilder Series Poetry Book Prize. Her poems have been published in literary magazines and journals that include *Indiana Voice Journal, The Indianapolis Review, Flying Island, The Asian American Literary Review*, and *The Rain, Party, & Disaster Society*. She loves to contemplate the oddities of life, such as mismatched buttons, abandoned houses, and birdsong in thunderstorms.

PAULA YUP returned to Spokane, WA after a dozen years in the Marshall Islands. In the past forty years she has published over two hundred poems in magazines and anthologies, including those from Outrider Press. Her first book of poetry is *Making a Clean Space in the Sky* (Evening Street Press).

ARE YOU KIDDING? (cont from inside front cover)

Eventually, I lost Mom. Though Mom lived in Georgia, she and I maintained a healthy communication. We exchanged letters and holiday cards. We talked on the phone at least once a month. She even came to visit in 1987. Then things began to change. *** Suddenly, her letters arrived more sporadically. And then, the "Phone Games."

The phone games began around 2005. *** By this time, the phone system was automated. The computer put me on hold while it gave Mom instructions on how to accept my call. About a minute later, the curt voice of the computer kicked in.

"Your call was not accepted. Please try again later." A few weeks later, I called Mom again. She accepted my call this time. Beginning our conversation, she asserted, "l heard you called a few weeks ago, but I was not here." Knowing she lived alone, I guessed, "I must have heard your answering machine." Caught off guard she blurted, "l don't have an answering machine." My mind went blank. I did not understand, but I was afraid to press farther.

As a dutiful son, I continued to go to that blue phone and enter her number every month. *** This continued until she died, May 3, 2007.

Then I lost my Dad. Though we had a tumultuous relationship in my youth because of his verbal abuse, Dad became my best friend. He was there for me from the very beginning.

He visited me twice a week while I was in county jail. And even though he was 71 when I was arrested, he continued to visit me faithfully regardless

(cont on inside back cover)